Women Who Followed Jesus

Women Who Followed Jesus

40 Devotions on the Journey to Easter

DANDI DALEY MACKALL

PARACLETE PRESS
Brewster, Massachusetts

2024 First Printing

Women Who Followed Jesus: 40 Devotions on the Journey to Easter

ISBN 978-1-64060-851-1

Library of Congress Control Number: 2023942394

10 9 8 7 6 5 4 3 2 1

Published by Paraclete Press
Brewster, Massachusetts
www.paracletepress.com

Cover design: Paraclete Design

Printed in India

For Jesus:

Let the words of my mouth and the meditation of my heart be acceptable to you,
O Lord, my rock and my redeemer.

—Psalm 19:14

CONTENTS

Author's Note 9

DAY 1 Mary Magdalene | *Despair* 13
DAY 2 Mary Magdalene | *Voices* 19
DAY 3 Mary Magdalene | *Light* 24
DAY 4 Mary, Mother of Jesus | *Sheep* 31
DAY 5 Mary, Mother of Jesus | *Love* 35
DAY 6 Susanna | *Touched* 43
DAY 7 Mary, Mother of Jesus | *Home* 48
DAY 8 Mary, Mother of Jesus | *Rejection* 53
DAY 9 Mary Magdalene | *Condemnation* 58
DAY 10 Joanna, Wife of Chuza | *Healing* 65
DAY 11 Joanna, Wife of Chuza | *Giving* 70
DAY 12 Samaritan Woman | *Living Water* 77
DAY 13 Samaritan Woman | *Testimony* 82
DAY 14 Mary of Bethany | *Hospitality* 89
DAY 15 Mary of Bethany | *Listening* 94
DAY 16 Mary of Bethany | *Waiting* 99
DAY 17 Martha | *Life* 105
DAY 18 Salome | *Ambition* 111
DAY 19 Salome | *Misplaced Boldness* 116
DAY 20 Joanna, Wife of Chuza | *Triumph* 121
DAY 21 Mary of Bethany | *Devotion* 126

THREE RELIGIOUS TRIALS 133

DAY 22 Joanna, Wife of Chuza | *Betrayed* 136
DAY 23 Mary Magdalene | *Empathy* 139

THREE ROMAN POLITICAL TRIALS 143

DAY 24 Mary Magdalene | Injustice 146
DAY 25 Mary Magdalene | Sorrow 149
DAY 26 Mary, Mother of Jesus | *Agony* 155
DAY 27 Mary Magdalene | *Seeking* 161

JESUS' SEVEN WORDS FROM THE CROSS 167

DAY 28 Salome | *Forgive* 171
DAY 29 Susanna | *Paradise-Bound* 175
DAY 30 Mary, Mother of Jesus | *Provision* 181
DAY 31 Mary of Bethany | *Forsaken* 186
DAY 32 Samaritan Woman | *Thirst* 191
DAY 33 Mary of Bethany | *Finished* 196
DAY 34 Mary, Mother of Jesus | *Spirit* 203
DAY 35 Joanna, Wife of Chuza | *Torn* 208
DAY 36 Mary Magdalene | *Loyalty* 214
DAY 37 Mary Magdalene | *Resurrection!* 221
DAY 38 Mary Magdalene | *Witnesses* 226
DAY 39 Mary, Mother of Jesus | *Peace* 231
DAY 40 Women Who Followed Jesus | *Purpose* 237

Afterword 247

Scripture Credits 249
For Further Study 251
About the Author 253

AUTHOR'S NOTE

And the sheep hear his voice. He calls his own sheep by name and leads them out. When he has brought out all his own, he goes ahead of them, and the sheep follow him because they know his voice. I am the good shepherd. The good shepherd lays down his life for the sheep." (John 10:3–4, 11)

I admit, I don't always read author letters, but I had to write this one for the sake of the rest of the book (and for my own sake). Would you mind reading it before jumping in? (If you're still with me, thank you!)

I want to say right up front that the only real truth we know for sure about these amazing women comes through Bible Scriptures, the verses that begin each day's reading. Each devotion attempts to tell the story of Jesus from the point of view of women whose lives he changed. With the exception of Jesus' mother and a couple of the others, we are given little information about the faithful women who traveled with Jesus as disciples, stayed through the Crucifixion, and were the first witnesses of the Resurrection. That tells us a lot of what we need to know about them: their love for Jesus, their faith and loyalty, their bravery, and their sacrifices.

Some of the women are called by name in Luke 8:1–3:

Soon afterward he [Jesus] went on through one town and village after another, proclaiming and bringing the good news of the kingdom of God. The twelve were with him, as well as some women who had been cured of evil spirits and infirmities: Mary, called Magdalene, from whom seven demons had gone out, and Joanna, the wife of Herod's steward Chuza, and Susanna, and many others, who ministered to them out of their own resources.

We're also given wonderful scenes of the Bethany sisters, Mary and Martha, in Luke 10:38–39:

Now as they went on their way, he [Jesus] entered a certain village where a woman named Martha welcomed him. She had a sister named Mary, who sat at Jesus's feet and listened to what he was saying.

I couldn't resist including a couple of women who, apparently, didn't join the travelers, but were profoundly changed by encounters with Christ.

These women narrate the events we celebrate at Easter. Their reports reveal their own lives as they speak—just as in my previous book, *Three Wise Women: 40 Devotions Celebrating Advent with Mary, Elizabeth, and Anna.*

I studied background material, various roles of first-century women, historical references about Jerusalem and the Temple, Galilee, Judea, and villages they would have walked through or stayed in, such as Capernaum, Nazareth, and Bethany. I've relied on Scripture and cultural details to further characterize each woman (Jewish, Galilean, Roman, Samaritan), as well as the historical and cultural setting of the times, crucifixions, and burials. And I've prayed, fearful that readers might take my Scripture-based imaginings as Scripture. This is why I urge you to focus on Scripture and celebrate Easter, while appreciating the faithful women disciples.

Have a great and wondrous Easter!

Dandi Daley Mackall

MARY MAGDALENE

Despair

. . . He [Jesus] *got into a boat with His disciples and sailed away. Upon their arrival in Dalmanutha* in the district of Magdala, *they were met by Pharisees—ready with their questions and tests—seeking some sign from heaven* that His teaching was from God.

(Mark 8:10–11, VOICE)

Soon afterward he went on through one town and village after another, proclaiming and bringing the good news of the kingdom of God. The twelve were with him, as well as some women who had been cured of evil spirits and infirmities: ***Mary, called Magdalene,*** *from whom seven demons had gone out . . . and many others. . . .*

(Luke 8:1–3)

You know how I am scorned, disgraced and shamed; all my enemies are before you. Scorn has broken my heart and has left me helpless; I looked for sympathy, but there was none, for comforters, but I found none.

(Psalm 69:19–20, NIV)

MARY MAGDALENE
Despair

I awake alone in darkness, my bed a rough mixture of dirt, rock, and unkempt grasses. I listen to the sounds of my village, Magdala, and to shouts of fishermen, already coming in from the Sea of Galilee. Starlings circle with a pair of coots, waiting for fishing boats with the night's catch.

Once when I woke beside the sea, I heard the one they call Jesus. A crowd had formed, and the man spoke from a fishermen's boat, words I had heard from a wild man called John the Baptist. "Repent, for the kingdom of God is near!" I had heard of Jesus, the man some call "Healer." Others whisper that he is the Messiah, come to free the Jewish nation from Roman domination. I care not for politics, and no man can give me freedom.

I pull myself to sit, and my head swims with the odor of alcohol, fish, and salt, Magdala's trademarks: fish and preservative industry. A sparrowhawk glides so nearby that if it had been a vulture, I would have been breakfast.

I lean against a fig tree that must have stopped my descent into the sea, for the hill is steep. I bear the scratches and cuts of someone who has tumbled over shrubs and rocks. When I attempt to recall the events of last night, or last day, a wave of nausea rises. *Why would I wish to remember anything?*

I get to my feet and notice that one sandal is missing. I am a spectator of myself, viewed from afar. Often I feel as if others inhabit my flesh and bones, leaving me with no self-control and little memory. Were I to name the residents of my mind, I would begin with "Accuser," "Controller," "Hope Thief," "Pain," and "Despair." Every conscious moment, these strangers rail against me, shaming me, robbing me of all hope, then taking control so I give in to urges.

I scan the terrain as I make my way up the ragged slope, a tower of rocks mocking my ascent. I curse when a sharp rock stabs my un-sandaled foot. By the time I reach the center of Magdala, I burn with a yearning so deep I cannot identify it. Someone—inside or outside my head—laughs when I stumble and fall to my knees.

An elderly woman limps toward me, then pauses to rub her malformed leg. Her faded blue tunic may have fit her when Herod was a child. For a moment, I think she is coming to my aid, recognizing me as a fellow outcast, and I wonder if the so-called Healer could fix her leg.

• • •

The old woman shuffles to me, her eyes reflecting a death-like flatness, devoid of compassion—I am well familiar with this look. She spits on the ground, near my bare foot. "God should strike you down! You are a disgrace to every righteous woman in Israel."

"Do you know of such a woman in Israel? Surely, there is none before me." I stand, bruised hands on battered hips.

The righteous woman, sputtering hate, storms off like a frightened fly released from the spider's web.

PONDERING . . .

1.) What is scorn? Have you ever felt scorned or the victim of gossip? Have you ever, even in your heart, scorned another person or group of people?

2.) Is there anything that makes you feel hopeless—even a small worry—about yourself, a loved one, or the world? Paul wrote to the Romans: *And hope does not put us to shame, because God's love has been poured out into our hearts through the Holy Spirit, who has been given to us (Romans 5:5).* How can God's love help you hope this Easter season?

3.) Is there a difference between hopelessness and despair? Have you ever tried to "snap out of it," to pull yourself out of despair? Which attempts helped, and which didn't?

4.) What help could you offer to someone you suspect may be hopeless or despairing? What could you say to that person? What would keep you from acting on your good intentions?

Dear God,
Help me place my hope in you
and keep it there every hour of every day.

MARY MAGDALENE

Voices

The voice of the LORD is powerful.

(Psalm 29:4)

"I am the good shepherd; I know my sheep and my sheep know me."

(John 10:14, NIV)

The voice of the LORD causes the oaks to whirl and strips the forest bare, and in his temple all say, "Glory!"

(Psalm 29:9)

But because of his great love for us, God, who is rich in mercy, made us alive with Christ even when we were dead in transgressions—it is by grace you have been saved.

(Ephesians 2:4–5, NIV)

MARY MAGDALENE

Voices

My footsteps—*slap, shush, slap, shush*—slow as I pass Magdala's main tavern.

"Magdalene! Come on in!" This voice, loaded with a jolliness borne of strong drink, belongs to a man whose "fun" turns into violence as fast as one drink turns into ten.

I determine to keep walking, but self-control lies beyond my reach. The voices in my head whisper, one swearing that a single drink can lighten the pain and guilt of life.

I enter the dark tavern, where unskilled music and lantern shadows welcome me back. One drink from a cup placed in my hand, and I am swaying across the dirty floor until I bump into a band of men. They smell of the sea, and neither they nor the few women with them look as though they are friends of strong drink. I recognize several of these fishermen of Galilee.

It is not until I look to the one who appears to be their leader that I recognize this man as he who spoke from the fishermen's boat. I cannot look away from his steady gaze, though nothing in his demeanor suggests he desires what other men seek.

"You are Mary of Magdala," he says, with the same commanding tone as by the sea.

Someone slurring words shouts, “He’s the one who made wine at the wedding in Cana with nothing but water. Likely a friend of yours, Magdalene.” The room fills with nervous laughter, then grows quiet. The voices in my head shout harsh words that turn to growls.

I want to ask Jesus if he is the Messiah, but a *stranger* in me will not let words pass my lips. I press my palms against my head to stop the roaring. A slice of darkness shoves me toward the door, and I obey, running through the women, stumbling outside, where black clouds cover the sky and sink into my head.

“Magdalene?” Jesus has followed me. “Mary of Magdala.” His words are a soft breeze that feels like arms around my soul. “I know you,” he says.

“NO!” The voice comes from me but does not sound like me. “Leave us!” Again, the words are not mine; for as much as I fear being disappointed once again, I want to believe there can be salvation, a freedom for someone like me.

Strangers inside of me are gearing up for war . . . and making me their shield.

PONDERING . . .

1.) Is there a situation in your life where your self-control isn't working? How can you let Jesus control it—and you—instead? What would that look like?

2.) You may not admit to hearing "voices" in your head, but do stray thoughts ever take over your mind with thoughts you know aren't from God? Ponder and pray about what you might do to get rid of them.

3.) The apostle Paul confessed in his letter to the Romans: *For I know that the good does not dwell within me, that is, in my flesh. For the desire to do the good lies close at hand, but not the ability* (Romans 7:18). Do you ever go through this kind of struggle?

4.) Later in his letter to the Romans, Paul writes that the answer to our inadequacy to do the good we want to do is "Jesus Christ our Lord." How is Jesus the answer to inner struggles? Ponder Mary of Magdala's struggle.

Dear God,
Thank you for freeing me from the power of sin.
Help me hear your voice.

MARY MAGDALENE

Light

It is you who light my lamp;
the Lord, my God, lights up my darkness.

(Psalm 18:28)

The Lord is my light and my salvation; whom shall I fear? The Lord is the stronghold of my life; of whom shall I be afraid?

(Psalm 27:1)

For with you is the fountain of life;
in your light we see light.

(Psalm 36:9)

The people who walked in darkness have seen a great light; those who lived in a land of deep darkness—on them light has shined.

(Isaiah 9:2)

MARY MAGDALENE
Light

I face Jesus, my gaze as intent as his, and I see light. I want that light, his peace . . . his salvation.

"Magdalene, I know the strangers that dwell in you, the demons that keep you in bondage. I am far stronger than they are because my Father is in me, and I am in him."

For an instant, my head clears, and I see a flicker of light, a way out, like the path through the Red Sea when Moses led the Israelites out of bondage in Egypt.

"Come out!" Jesus demands. But the army within me aims and fires. I scream, then feel hands on my shoulders. Jesus shouts, "Come out of this poor woman!"

I think I am being ripped apart so completely that I crumble to the ground, onto the feet of Jesus. He touches my head. "By the power of Elohim, the All-Powerful One, be gone!"

I don't want this glimmer of hope. And yet I want the whole. Pain shoots through my entire body, and I wonder if this is what the dying must endure.

With one jagged burst of pain, the strangers have left me at the feet of Jesus the Messiah. I see myself and my life of sin. "Oh, Jesus, please forgive me!" The pain of seeing my sin is worse than the physical pain.

"Mary of Magdala, you are forgiven," Jesus says. "And you are loved."

Loved? Forgiven? I look at the sweet expressions on the faces of the good men and women with Jesus. "I will never be good enough, Rabbi."

An older woman, her tunic showing the dust of their journey, smiles as she helps me to my feet. "I am Mary, mother of Jesus. Isaiah himself said that no one is good, not even one. It is faith that rescues us."

Others draw closer, smiling, joyful. A lovely young woman introduces me to the fisherman I once saw by Lake Gennesaret. "This is Simon, my husband. I mean Peter. Jesus changed his name."

A woman whose gaze rests on two men young enough to be her sons, calls to them, "James! John!" as only a mother would.

An unfamiliar lightness washes over me. If this is freedom, then I shall give my thanks and live in it forever and ever.

PONDERING . . .

1.) Do you remember a clear-cut moment when you accepted Christ's salvation? If yes, reflect on what led you to that moment of belief. If not, can you track your journey to knowing Christ?

2.) How strongly did you feel your need for forgiveness when you came to Christ? If you came to Christ as a child, have you ever struggled with keeping that childlike faith?

3.) What's the biggest temptation for you to wander from Christ? What are some of the main reasons you never want to stop growing in your relationship with Jesus?

4.) Jesus is the Light, shows us the light, guides us with his light. In what ways do you sense "light" from Jesus day to day?

Dear God,
Thank you for shining your light
on the path ahead.

MARY, MOTHER OF JESUS

Sheep

When he has brought out all his own,
he goes ahead of them, and the sheep follow him
because they know his voice.

(John 10:4)

". . . I have come that they may have life, and have it to the full. I am the good shepherd. The good shepherd lays down his life for the sheep."

(John 10:10–11, NIV)

He will feed his flock like a shepherd; he will gather the lambs in his arms and carry them in his bosom and gently lead the mother sheep.

(Isaiah 40:11)

Mary, Mother of Jesus

Sheep

My son continually amazes me. It is a gift to watch Jesus as he transforms this woman, Mary of Magdala, from spiritual death to eternal life. How I wish my Joseph were still alive and could see what Jesus is doing! How proud he would have been! I know this incredible plan of salvation comes from my son's heavenly Father, but Jesus' earthly father fulfilled his role with love and faithfulness.

The lines in the face of Magdalene release and become smooth, and I can no longer resist the urge to hug my new sister. I put my arms around her and sense her body stiffen, then ease. "When Jesus sets you free," I whisper, "you are free forever, Magdalene." Her bruised face glows with the truth of my words, and her eyes widen as a child's.

"Tell us what it was like," Salome demands. She takes sandals from Susanna's outstretched hand, then kneels to put them on the feet of Magdalene. The gesture is lovely, though I am less sure of Salome's inquiry.

"Magdalene may not yet be ready to share her life with us," I say.

"I cannot take so fine a sandal on so filthy a foot," Magdalene protests.

Salome ignores the refusal while Susanna whisks a sky-colored tunic from her travel bag and places it around Magdalene's shoulders. I know Susanna has great wealth, but her quiet generosity overflows. And yet, something within her keeps her distant.

I nod to our friend and benefactor. "Susanna, too, has come to believe. Jehovah-Jireh, the Great Provider, sent her to us at just the right time."

Salome sits back on her heels. "So? What happened?"

Magdalene's eyes close, and I almost tell Salome to stop asking questions. But when Magdalene opens her eyes, they are filled with wonder and joy. "I heard Jesus."

Susanna's head tilts, freeing a strand of hair from her long, shiny black braid. "I, too, was healed by Jesus."

Jesus joins us, and Magdalene turns to him. "I heard you. For years, I have heard the voices shaming me, urging me to sin, screaming inside my head. They blocked every other sound and left me empty. But I heard you. The only voice I heard was yours."

Jesus gives her the smile I have lived for each day of his life, a piece of joy, filled with light and delight. "Of course you heard me! I am the Good Shepherd. I know my sheep, and they know me. My sheep hear my voice and follow me."

Magdalene glances at her new sandals. "Follow you?" Her countenance shines as she declares, "Yes! I will follow you."

PONDERING . . .

1.) In John 10, Jesus calls himself the Shepherd and calls us his sheep. Ponder the ways this applies to your relationship with Christ. How can we know we're following the right voice?

2.) How do you hear Jesus' voice? Can you recall specific moments or events when you believe you heard his voice? How did you know the words, or thoughts, came from God?

3.) What other voices vie for your attention? What thoughts take up too much space in your head? What can you do to discern Jesus' voice above all the other voices?

4.) In Psalm 95:7, David says: *For he is our God, and we are the people of his pasture and the sheep of his hand. O that today you would listen to his voice!* Close your eyes and sit in silence for a few minutes, asking God to help you listen to what he's saying to you today.

Dear God,
Please help me hear the voice of my Shepherd.

MARY, MOTHER OF JESUS

Love

We love because he first loved us.

(1 John 4:19)

Whoever does not love does not know God,
for God is love.

(1 John 4:8)

Let me hear of your steadfast love in the morning,
for in you I put my trust. Teach me the way I should
go, for to you I lift up my soul.

(Psalm 143:8)

O give thanks to the LORD, for he is good,

for his steadfast love endures forever.

(Psalm 136:1)

How precious is your steadfast love, O God! All people may take refuge in the shadow of your wings.

(Psalm 36:7)

Mary, Mother of Jesus

Love

On the hard, dusty path ahead of me, Magdalene sings in a voice that reminds me of a courtyard gate my Joseph, an excellent carpenter, never got around to fixing. I recognize the psalm being sung, though not the key or tune behind the words. Often, we have all sung together on our journey to Capernaum, also known as "Adonai's Playground," where grapes, olives, and walnuts dot blankets of green, and the scent of the sea penetrates my soul.

Now, making our way to Jerusalem for Passover, only Magdalene sings, for none of us share the key of Magdalene.

"Magdalene, please?" This is not the first plea from Peter, which always earns him a sweet and mischievous grin. She elbows him and is rewarded with Peter's reluctant grin as she begins a Sabbath Day psalm: "It is good to give thanks to the Lord, to sing praises to your name, O Most High!"

Dust wedges between my toes as I struggle to keep pace with Magdalene, Salome, and the boys. When I glance over at Jesus, I am rewarded with the joy of his countenance. Sunlight illuminates his too-long hair. The neck of his tunic is frayed, and the hem tattered. I must make him a new tunic when I return to Nazareth.

"All is well, I trust?" Jesus asks, though he knows.

True, I am getting on in years, but I can still climb every hill in Galilee. "And why should it not be well, my son?"

For my answer, I receive an impish grin that reminds me of running races with my little Jesus, letting him win—and again, later, when he let me win.

Magdalene stops singing, throws back her head, and breathes in sunlight as if she has never before felt such a thing. "Oh, Mary, how much your son loves you!"

I fear she has little experience in being loved. "Jesus loves all of us with no conditions. Jesus loves you, Mary of Magdala."

"Move aside!" A carriage forces us off the road. The men inside are Sadducees, judging by their fine white linen garments and turbans, their crafted ephods wrapped at the waist. "Prostitutes traveling with men? You should be jailed or worse."

They are gone, but their scorn lingers, and I see the weight of accusations heavy on Magdalene. "Are you all right?"

"Do I still deserve condemnation when, for the first time, I am doing nothing wrong?"

"I know. How the gossip against Joseph and me plagued us and our families!"

"Why would those religious leaders be so vicious? I hate them, Mary."

I take her hand, and we resume walking. "I understand. Their words cut like sharpened stones. But they do not need hate. They need love. And Jesus loves them."

She is silent for a time, then starts singing: "How precious is your steadfast love, O God! All people may take refuge in the shadow of your wings."

I join my sister in song.

PONDERING . . .

1.) Psalms are songs, and singing was central to worship in biblical times. After the Last Supper, Jesus and the disciples sang a hymn before going to the Mount of Olives. How can singing deepen your celebrations this Easter?

2.) Jesus journeyed with a diverse group of men and women, traveling over rough terrain, often sleeping on the ground or in close quarters. What kinds of disagreements or problems might have come up? How do you handle difficulties when they occur in your family or church?

3.) Religious leaders were quick to believe the worst about Jesus' band of men and women disciples. Do you think Christians sometimes judge others or assume the worst? Do you?

4.) Have you ever been falsely accused, or the victim of gossip? What did you do about it? What did you feel like doing? Ponder what you will do the next time you hear gossip, even about someone you dislike.

Dear God,
Help me to sing your praises all day long!

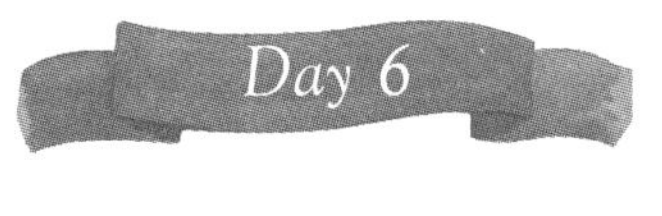

SUSANNA

Touched

Soon afterward he went on through one town and village after another, proclaiming and bringing the good news of the kingdom of God. The twelve were with him, as well as some women who had been cured of evil spirits and infirmities: Mary, called Magdalene, from whom seven demons had gone out, and Joanna, the wife of Herod's steward Chuza, and ***Susanna****, and many others, who ministered to them out of their own resources.*

(Luke 8:1–3)

Just then there came a man named Jairus, a leader of the synagogue. He fell at Jesus's feet and began pleading with him to come to his house, for he had an only daughter, about twelve years old, and she was dying.

(Luke 8:41–42a)

As he [Jesus] *went, the crowds pressed in on him. Now there was a woman who had been suffering from a flow of blood for twelve years, and though she had spent all she had on physicians, no one could cure her. She came up behind him and touched the fringe of his cloak, and immediately her flow of blood stopped. Then Jesus asked, "Who touched me?"*

(Luke 8:42b–45)

Susanna
Touched

"Susanna?" Magdalene calls to me from the front of the crowd following Jesus.

I am surprised to be missed. Magdalene and the others have been kind to me, although Salome is a bit like hair in my teeth, irritating, though not with intent. The truth is I rarely feel I am part of these disciples. They are bold in speech and skilled in service to the group. I long to contribute more than occasional provisions.

The road is filled with rich and poor, all hoping to see a miracle. We were by the sea when a synagogue leader, Jairus, ran up and fell at Jesus' feet and cried, "My little daughter is dying. Please come make her well!"

I am almost to Magdalene when I notice a woman ahead of me shrouded in her black tunic, her face covered, save for eyes drained of life. Someone bumps into me, and I lose sight of the woman until she reappears close behind Jesus. She bends, then almost instantly, rises with a vigor I would not have thought possible.

I collide with the Pharisee ahead of me, as he stops suddenly. Ahead of him, Jesus has stopped. Beside him, Jairus shifts from foot to foot as Jesus surveys the crowd.

Jesus shouts, "Who touched my cloak?"

All around come the denials: "Not I, Sir!" "No." "We are too distant." "I never!" "Not me." Some near the Messiah step back.

Finally, Peter asks what all must be thinking, including myself. "Master, the crowds are hemming you in and pressing against you." Others with him nod in confused agreement. "How can you ask who touched you?"

Jesus studies the crowd. "Someone touched me. I perceived power had gone out from me."

The shrouded woman cowering beneath a spreading oak steps out, trembling. "Lord, I touched you. I have suffered for twelve years from a continuous issue of blood."

Several in the crowd gasp. This condition renders her unclean, along with anyone she touched. "I gave everything I had to physicians, who performed blood-letting and every supposed cure, from making me confess my sin to forcing me to drink expensive potions. Nothing worked! My money is gone as are family and friends. But the instant I touched the fringe of your garment, I was healed. Praise to Adonai, who has sent his Son!"

As she speaks, I feel as if I know her. Though I have no share in her suffering, not since Jesus healed my illness, I know her isolation and lack of community. But as she praises Jesus for his compassion and healing touch, I share in this also.

PONDERING . . .

1.) If you've experienced long-term pain or suffering, what effect has it had on you? On those around you?

2.) What can you say to someone (even to yourself) when you pray God will take away the pain, but it doesn't happen? Is there someone who is suffering right now, a person you could try to comfort?

3.) Could Jesus have healed everyone at the same time? Why do you think he didn't? Do you believe God could take away your pain or that of a loved one in an instant?

4.) How does medical science fit with faith in God's healing power? Do you believe God can use others as instruments of healing, even if they may not realize it?

Dear God,
Show me how you can use me
to help those who are suffering.

Day 7

MARY, MOTHER OF JESUS

Home

He left that place and came to his hometown, and his disciples followed him. On the Sabbath he began to teach in the synagogue, and many who heard him were astounded. They said, "Where did this man get all this? What is this wisdom that has been given to him? What deeds of power are being done by his hands! Is not this the carpenter, the son of Mary and brother of James and Joses and Judas and Simon, and are not his sisters here with us?" And they took offense at him. Then Jesus said to them, "Prophets are not without honor, except in their hometown and among their own kin and in their own house." And he could do no deed of power there, except that he laid his hands on a few sick people and cured them. And he was amazed at their unbelief.

(Mark 6:1–6)

Jesus replied, "Foxes have dens. Birds have nests. But the Son of Man has no place to lay his head."

(Matthew 8:20, NIrV)

Mary, Mother of Jesus
Home

Word from Herod's palace has reached us that Elizabeth's son, John, is dead, beheaded by Herod at the whim of his wife. I have continued to grieve the passing of dear Elizabeth, and now for her son. Jesus believed no better man lived upon the earth. Now my son works even harder to carry the message of repentance and salvation to every village.

This day we shall reach Nazareth; my soul rejoices. I wake Magdalene and Salome when stars still poke through the sky. While Salome builds a fire from the night's smoldering logs, I empty the last of the lentils into a pan. "Magdalene, I would like you to sing, please." Though she knows my purpose, she begins with the eagerness of a child.

Early on the third day as we near the familiar hills of the south, Magdalene trots up and places a fat cucumber slice between my teeth. Its coolness soothes my dry lips and slakes my thirst. "Mary, you must be pleased to return home, yes?"

It is a deep longing. "I shall cook until even both Bartholomew and Philip are filled. Nazareth is a small village with just one synagogue, so you will be welcomed by the entire community."

Nathanael rushes past, snatching a cucumber slice from Magdalene's bowl. "Can any good thing come out of

Nazareth?" This is not the first time he has repeated the old proverb, one deserving of the swat I give his arm.

Perched on a hill overlooking the Esdraelon plain, we watch travelers from Jerusalem and Egypt. Colorful caravans, as if from another world, pass on trade routes below. Tall firs guard the village but allow us to cross into the valley between Nazareth and Cana, where clusters of yellow mustard seed and wildflowers gather amid twisted acacia and olive trees. A tiny flock of geese flies in a V above us, their honking not unlike the Shofar at temple. Every corner of Nazareth holds memories . . . though not all are good.

We gather onlookers as Jesus leads us through the center of Nazareth, past the olive press, to our home, where we are a tight fit. Our Lord honors us with his creativity at sunset as we eat in the courtyard, the aroma of fish and spices floating in a winding trail of smoke. Afterward, Jesus and I walk around the village as Joseph and I loved doing so long ago.

"Now, Jesus, tomorrow in synagogue you must stand tall when you read from the scroll, though you may sit to answer questions. Please do not cause an uproar by looking for someone to heal until we have left the synagogue."

My son gazes at the harvested barley field, then breathes in the sky. "I have been to synagogue before, Mother." We exchange grins and the silence of the familiar as we walk home.

Pondering . . .

1.) How do you feel when you think of your hometown or childhood home? Do you think your recollections are always accurate? Explain.

2.) Have you gone to any school reunions? How badly did you want—or *not* want—to attend? Name specific changes in the way you view certain classmates . . . and yourself.

3.) Do you think it's true that a "prophet" is without honor in his hometown? Do you feel appreciated in your hometown? Your home? Family? Church?

4.) What influence did your hometown have on you? Ponder your current "hometown." What can you do this Easter to make life better where you live?

Dear God,
Thank you for my hometown,
even with its flaws . . . and mine.

MARY, MOTHER OF JESUS

Rejection

When he came to Nazareth, where he had been brought up, he went to the synagogue on the Sabbath day, as was his custom. He stood up to read, and the scroll of the prophet Isaiah was given to him. He unrolled the scroll and found the place where it was written:

"The Spirit of the Lord is upon me,
because he has anointed me to bring good news to the poor. He has sent me to proclaim release to the captives and recovery of sight to the blind,
to set free those who are oppressed,
to proclaim the year of the Lord's favor."

And he rolled up the scroll, gave it back to the attendant, and sat down. The eyes of all in the synagogue were fixed on him. Then he began to say to them, "Today this Scripture has been fulfilled in your hearing."

(Luke 4:16–21)

And he said, "Truly I tell you, no prophet is accepted in his hometown."

(Luke 4:24)

He was despised and rejected by mankind, a man of suffering, and familiar with pain. Like one from whom people hide their faces he was despised, and we held him in low esteem.

(Isaiah 53:3, NIV)

Mary, Mother of Jesus

Rejection

Neighbors who have insulted me for my unusual pregnancy now honor us with the best seats in the synagogue. Shafts of light burst through the windows to the stone arch where Jesus will stand. Many from Nazareth must listen from outside.

Salome leans across Susanna and whispers, "James and John are right next to Jesus."

The crowd quiets as the scroll is handed to Jesus. He reads from Isaiah: "The spirit of the Lord God is upon me because the Lord has anointed me; he has sent me to bring good news to the oppressed, to bind up the brokenhearted." It is a well-known Messianic passage. As Jesus continues, heads nod, for all Israel hopes for a Messiah who will overthrow the Romans.

Murmurs of approval reverberate as Jesus rolls up the scroll and hands it to the attendant. But I sense my son is not finished. "Today this Scripture has been fulfilled in your hearing."

Suddenly, the air in the synagogue turns stale, the breeze evaporates, and my heart threatens to stop beating. Men exchange hardened frowns, brows furrowed. "Wait! Is this not Joseph's son?" From the women's gallery, whispers buzz like angry wasps.

"You say, 'Do here the things you did in Capernaum,' but no prophet is accepted in his hometown." Jesus must shout to be heard above the rage, which increases when he points out that Elijah was sent to a widow in Sidon, not Israel, and only Naaman the Syrian was cleansed of leprosy, though Israel had many lepers.

Men spring to their feet, fists raised. Old Japheth cries, "Is he saying God loves Gentiles, foreigners, and not Israel?" The rabbi shouts, "The Messiah will save Israel from foreigners!"

I see my son, his face fearless as the mob drags him out of the synagogue to the top of the hill on which our village sits. "Stop!" I scream. But we are all trapped by sweaty bodies, male and female, their stench sickening, hands slippery as their minds. They intend to hurl my child, the Son of God, their Savior, over the cliff. I cannot watch this madness. Dear El Roi, "the God who sees," please stop them from—!

Then as suddenly as the crowd turned in the synagogue, they stop, their shouts silenced. I fear that in their ignorance and unbelief, they have killed my Jesus. I feel Magdalene's arms holding me up as my bones melt and knees give way.

"Mary, look." Magdalene's rough palm lifts my chin, and I see my son—alive, head raised, eyes sad—not for himself, but for the mob he now walks through.

Jesus passes in the midst of them as they can only stare in wonder at the Messiah they have rejected.

PONDERING . . .

1.) Have you ever been openly, or subtly, rejected? If you've been rejected by a friend, or friends, what did you do? In retrospect, would you have handled it in a different way?

2.) Jesus used kindly Gentiles, non-Israelites, and foreigners as the "good guys" in certain parables, such as the Good Samaritan. He healed many who were not from Israel and welcomed them as followers. What is your feeling about people not like you or not born in your country?

3.) Why do you think the people of Nazareth rejected Jesus? Are you rejecting anyone or any group of people? If you're with others who reject someone with words or actions, what do you do? What should you do?

4.) Describe some of the different forms rejection can take. Ponder the impact rejection can have. How does the story of Easter help?

Dear God,
Give me your compassion for
people I feel like rejecting.
Heal my wounds of rejection.

MARY MAGDALENE

Condemnation

Early in the morning he [Jesus] came again to the temple. All the people came to him, and he sat down and began to teach them. The scribes and the Pharisees brought a woman who had been caught in adultery, and, making her stand before all of them, they said to him, "Teacher, this woman was caught in the very act of committing adultery. Now in the law Moses commanded us to stone such women. Now what do you say?" They said this to test him, so that they might have some charge to bring against him. Jesus bent down and wrote with his finger on the ground.

(John 8:2–6)

As far as the east is from the west, so far he removes our transgressions from us.

(Psalm 103:12)

Therefore there is now no condemnation for those who are in Christ Jesus.

(Romans 8:1)

MARY MAGDALENE
Condemnation

I miss Mary and would have stayed with her in Nazareth had she not urged me to journey with Jesus to Jerusalem for the Passover. At least, Mary, wife of Clopas, will be with her.

Salome and I stand apart from Jesus, who teaches at the entrance to the Court of the Gentiles. Pharisees, never without broad phylacteries on their foreheads and blue fringe rivaling one another in length, circle Jesus but gaze across Temple grounds as if expecting a storm.

"Why do people in Judea scorn Galileans?" I ask.

Salome sets down her basket. "We may as well be foreigners."

Her son James deepens his Galilean accent. "We live near pagan cities and break rules."

John nods. "As if the Torah did not give us ample rules—613, and thousands added to those by the Pharisees."

"Zebedee says they made thirty-nine categories of what work means in 'Don't work on the Sabbath,'" Salome explains. "How many steps I may take, letters I may write, and—"

"They're here!" A group of scribes are dragging a woman in the dirt to shove her in front of Jesus. My eyes burn at her filthy hair, meager tunic barely covering her bare and battered limbs. One Pharisee, his white tunic unsoiled, points to her. "Teacher, this woman was caught in the act of adultery! The

Law of Moses commands us to stone such a woman. What say you?"

It is a trap. I want Jesus to remind them that men are included in the Torah's condemnation. But he simply bends down and writes with his finger in the dust while the woman trembles and Pharisees demand an answer. Dust rises in sunlight as the men pick up stones.

When Jesus stands, it is as if Jerusalem holds its breath. "Let anyone among you who is without sin be the first to cast a stone." Again, he writes in dust.

I turn away, unable to watch this poor woman be torn apart by jagged stones hurled by self-righteous men.

Thunk! Plop! Plop, plop, plop! Plunk!

I turn back and see men dropping stones, then slinking away, oldest to youngest, leaving Jesus and the woman alone. "Woman, where are they? Has no one condemned you?" Jesus asks.

Her answer comes in a voice small as a grain of sand. "No one, Sir."

Jesus meets her gaze as if only she exists and he has journeyed from heaven just for her. "Go your way, and do not sin."

The tears that track her dirty cheeks might be mine. Her lips move without sound as she walks away, pausing once to glance over her shoulder at the One who forgives all.

Pondering . . .

1.) What sins in others do you find yourself pointing out and condemning? What sins do you accept as part of life now when years ago you never would have considered them okay?

2.) Which of your own sins do you tend not to worry about? Ponder the consequences of those "worry-free" sins.

3.) Do you tend to condemn the sinner with the sin? Jesus died for our sins so we will never be separated from God. But has sin ever made you feel separated, or distanced, from God?

4.) This Easter season, how could you show kindness and the love of Christ to someone, or to a group of people, you've been condemning in your heart?

Dear God,
Please keep me from condemning others,
even in my thoughts.

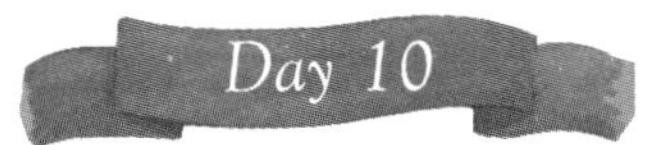

JOANNA, WIFE OF CHUZA

Healing

Soon afterward he went on through one town and village after another, proclaiming and bringing the good news of the kingdom of God. The twelve were with him, as well as some women who had been cured of evil spirits and infirmities: Mary, called Magdalene, from whom seven demons had gone out, and ***Joanna****, the wife of Herod's steward Chuza, and Susanna, and many others, who ministered to them out of their own resources.*

(Luke 8:1–3)

In the temple he found people selling cattle, sheep, and doves and the money changers seated at their tables. Making a whip of cords, he drove all of them out of the temple, with the sheep and the cattle. He also poured out the coins of the money changers and overturned their tables. He told those who were selling the doves, "Take these things out of here! Stop making my Father's house a marketplace!"

(John 2:14–16)

It is zeal for your house that has consumed me;
the insults of those who insult you have fallen on me.

(Psalm 69:9)

JOANNA, WIFE OF CHUZA
Healing

Chuza smooths a fold in the silk veil he has selected for our Passover worship, rose silk from China and cotton from India for my gown. My husband's role as epitropos for Herod Antipas includes serving as steward of Herod's domestic affairs and finances. His attention to palace dress often extends to my own. "Joanna, we must go to Temple."

We have traveled from Herod's palace in Tiberius to his palace-fortress here in Jerusalem. Now we weave through hundreds of pilgrims speaking dozens of languages. I do my best to keep up with Chuza, but my neck has turned to iron, and my knees rub bone upon bone as if starting a fire that travels my spine. My legs collapse, and I fall to the ground, crying out to Adonai, in whom I have believed since childhood. How I had hoped to see the Messiah here.

Shouts of the moneychangers and bleating of sacrificial lambs and cattle sound as desperate as I am. I cover my head as boots come at me.

A strong arm slips around me, lifting me to my feet. Expecting to see Chuza, I am transfixed by a man with eyes formed of hesed, of lovingkindness and mercy. "You are weary." His soft voice rises above all surrounding noise. "Do you believe I can heal you, Joanna?"

He knows my name? And somehow, I know this is Jesus, the one John the Baptizer called "Messiah." I return the gaze he has fixed upon me and answer, "Yes!"

"That's good." Smiling, Jesus releases me and steps back. "Because you are healed."

Chuza is by my side. I take his hands and circle in a wedding twirl. I turn to thank my Healer, and the Messiah is gone. "There, Joanna!" Chuza points to the tables that line the Court of the Gentiles, and I see Jesus carefully twisting cords into a whip.

A minute later, Jesus storms the Temple Court and overturns the tables of the cheating moneychangers, sending ill-gotten coins jangling. My heart cheers as he opens cages, freeing doves to celebrate the heavens, their wings applauding the winds like flights of angels. He frees the oft-deformed, sacrificial cattle and lambs, driving them out with the moneychangers. "Stop making my Father's house a marketplace!"

"It is zeal for your house that has consumed me; the insults of those who insult you have fallen on me." I repeat David's words, knowing the prophecy is before us.

PONDERING . . .

1.) Why do you think Jesus healed Joanna and the other women who journeyed with him, such as Mary Magdalene, Susanna, and others? Do you believe God still heals today?

2.) Have you ever asked to be healed of a malady that continues unchanged? Do you see that as unanswered prayer? The apostle Paul wrote about his "thorn in the flesh." He prayed for God to remove it, but he wasn't healed. He ends with, "For whenever I am weak, then I am strong" (2 Corinthians 12:7–10) How does that work?

3.) What could you say to a friend's bitterness at not having been healed, or of God's allowing a loved one to suffer?

4.) This Easter, ask God to show you someone who blames God for suffering. Listen without judging. Let God lead you and give you the words to say.

Dear God,
Help me to trust you as Healer
And to help others who are suffering.

Day 11

JOANNA, WIFE OF CHUZA

Giving

"Do not store up for yourselves treasures on earth, where moth and rust consume and where thieves break in and steal, but store up for yourselves treasures in heaven, where neither moth nor rust consumes and where thieves do not break in and steal. For where your treasure is, there your heart will be also."

(Matthew 6:19–21)

Each of you must give as you have made up your mind, not regretfully or under compulsion, for God loves a cheerful giver.

(2 Corinthians 9:7)

"Give, and it will be given to you. A good measure, pressed down, shaken together, running over, will be put into your lap, for the measure you give will be the measure you get back."

(Luke 6:38)

JOANNA, WIFE OF CHUZA
Giving

Two days have passed, and life in the palace is unbearable. I partake in society for Chuza's sake, but I find no joy in the display of my jewels and silks. Friends marvel that I am no longer in pain. Yet when I tell them Jesus healed me, they scoff or exchange looks of pity.

I know what I must do, and finally, I open my heart to my husband. "Chuza, I wish to take my personal jewels and coins to Jesus and those who journey with him."

Chuza's thick white eyebrows merge in rare anger. "Joanna, you may not! Men and women travel together—scandalous! If Herod found out and did not kill us, he would rid Israel of us, and we would need your personal wealth to survive. The answer is no."

Believing Elohim will change Chuza's heart, I begin packing my jewels into my kophinos, a basket not unlike Chuza's larger *kuphta*.

Several days pass before I see proof that Elohim has been at work. "Joanna, I will not prevent you from doing what the all-powerful Elohim commands." Chuza reminds me that I must not speak with a man in public. "I suppose I must send with you a tithe. A tenth of my earnings? What are Jesus' rules?"

I touch my husband's cheek. "Chuza, Jesus does not add rules. He changes hearts." At that moment I realize Jesus does not want my jewelry or my provisions—he wants me.

Before dawn and feeling no pain, I walk up the coast toward the rising sun, to the music of chirping crickets. Everyone I ask knows where Jesus and the disciples encamp. One wizened woman breaks into a huge grin. "Jesus healed me! He can heal you too."

Much later I hear loud laughter mixed with groans. The sun shifts, casting light across the rippling waves of the Sea of Galilee, illuminating a camp with four tents circling a campfire. People press toward the largest tent at the edge of camp. Children are everywhere—held by parents, joining hands with other children, running between tents.

A woman I have seen near the Temple meets me in long strides. "Welcome! Joanna, is it not? I am Mary of Magdala, though we have so many Marys, I am called Magdalene." Another, more aged, woman joins us. "I am Salome, and those unruly boys are my sons, James and John. Wherever you see Jesus, you will see the boys. Jesus said to expect you."

"He what?" I did not even know myself that I would be here.

Others join us, each with a story, a miracle, a belief. Magdalene hands my gifts to the one called Judas. He peers into my basket. "You are very generous! This Canaanite gold-winged pin from Mesopotamia . . . and these Carnelian gemstones inlaid with lapis lazuli?"

"My ancestors saved the heirlooms through exile and war." Seeing him handle my grandmother's treasures makes me wish I had held back something.

I am ashamed of this desire and hope that being near Jesus will change me.

Pondering . . .

1.) If you are single, how do you settle arguments with friends and family? If you're married, how do you and your spouse settle differences (like Chuza and Joanna)? Ponder the last time you didn't get your way.

2.) What do you consider your most valuable possession (an object rather than a person or spiritual possession—a thing)? What makes it valuable to you?

3.) We've all heard the adage, "You can't take it with you." Ponder things in your life that are visible and things that are invisible. What does it mean to you that only things you can take with you to eternity are invisible?

4.) What are you putting your security in? Savings for next month? Enough money for retirement and care in your old age? What would you do if you lost "everything"?

Dear God,
Help me trust you, and only you,
for my security.

SAMARITAN WOMAN

Living Water

So he came to a Samaritan city called Sychar, near the plot of ground that Jacob had given to his son Joseph. Jacob's well was there, and Jesus, tired out by his journey, was sitting by the well. It was about noon.

(John 4:5–6)

A Samaritan woman came to draw water, and Jesus said to her, "Give me a drink." (His disciples had gone to the city to buy food.) The Samaritan woman said to him, "How is it that you, a Jew, ask a drink of me, a woman of Samaria?" (Jews do not share things in common with Samaritans.) Jesus answered her, "If you knew the gift of God and who it is that is saying to you, 'Give me a drink,' you would have asked him, and he would have given you living water."

(John 4:7–10)

Hear, everyone who thirsts; come to the waters; and you who have no money, come, buy and eat! Come, buy wine and milk without money and without price.

(Isaiah 55:1)

SAMARITAN WOMAN
Living Water

Heat bears down on me like a fiery shawl melded to my shoulders. Other women of Sychar fetch water in the cool of the morning, a time I am not welcome. When the well comes into view, I am surprised to see a man sitting near it. Perhaps I should be afraid, but he can do to me no worse than other men have.

The man has the look of a pure Jew in his simple tunic tied at the waist, his hair reaching his shoulders. He is bold enough to pass through Samaria, rather than bypass our dangerous "heathen" population. Jews and Samaritans have hated each other for 700 years, since the Assyrians conquered the Northern Kingdom of Israel and forced intermarriage.

I return his stare. He grins, but the smile is not flirtatious. "Give me a drink."

His words shock me more than if he had suggested we swim together in the well. "How is it that you, a Jew, ask me for a drink?" Touching my jar would render him unclean. I have heard a rabbi's teaching: "The water of Samaria is more unclean than the blood of swine."

He laughs as though reading my thoughts. "If you knew the gift of God and who asks you for a drink, you would have asked him, and he would have given you living water."

Is this man flirting with me, or merely teasing, both arts at which I excel. "Sir, where do you get that living water? Are you greater than Jacob, who gave us this well?"

He continues as if I have not spoken. "Everyone who drinks of this water will be thirsty again, but those who drink of the water that I will give them will never be thirsty. The water that I will give will become in them a spring of water gushing up to eternal life."

"Sir, give me this water, so that I may never be thirsty or have to keep coming here to draw water." We are either flirting, or crazy. I see no such living water.

"Go, call your husband, and come back."

I knew it—another false promise. He is no prophet. "I have no husband."

He shows no embarrassment at being wrong. "You are right, for you have had five husbands, and the one you have now is not your husband!"

How can he know this? "Sir, I see you are a prophet, but we believe there have been no prophets since the death of Moses and until the return of Assaief, the Messiah."

His laughter is hearty, yet loving. "Dear woman, I who speak with you am the Messiah."

PONDERING . . .

1.) John writes that Jesus "had to go through Samaria." Jesus might easily have chosen the more popular route to bypass the hostile territory of Samaria. Have you ever felt led to do something you wouldn't normally do?

2.) Why do you think Jesus started his conversation with the Samaritan woman by asking for her help? How do you react when someone, especially someone you believe to be your critic, asks you for help?

3.) History had led Samaritans and Jews to despise each other. What automatic hatreds, or "suspicions," exist today? Do you recognize any prejudices in yourself? What could you do to help with today's *pre-judgments*?

4.) How would you define "living water"? Have you drunk the living water from Jesus? How would you explain "living water" to an unbeliever?

Dear God,
Thank you for the living water of
my salvation. Help me to be
continually grateful.

Day 13

SAMARITAN WOMAN

Testimony

Just then his disciples came. They were astonished that he was speaking with a woman, but no one said, "What do you want?" or "Why are you speaking with her?" Then the woman left her water jar and went back to the city. She said to the people, "Come and see a man who told me everything I have ever done! He cannot be the Messiah, can he?"

(John 4:27–29)

Many Samaritans from that city believed in him because of the woman's testimony, "He told me everything I have ever done."

(John 4:39)

"Let anyone who is thirsty come to me, and let the one who believes in me drink. As the Scripture has said, 'Out of the believer's heart shall flow rivers of living water.'"

(John 7:37–38)

SAMARITAN WOMAN
Testimony

God's Messiah has revealed himself to me. *Me!* I break into joyous laughter until I notice several men cautiously approaching. Jesus waves them over. Their faces are lined with disapproval. The Messiah speaking with a woman? A Samaritan?

"I'm off to tell my people." I leave the Messiah to make his own explanations.

I am dripping with sweat when I burst into the town square, packed with crowds seeking shade from the horseshoe of cedars. Servers pour wine from an amphora, a pointed jug, into large bowls, or kraters. Most of those gathered know enough of me to avoid me. Some frown as if unsure who stands smiling before them. "Listen! I have great news! I have met a man who—."

Laughter rumbles across the open square. "Always a man!" A wealthy landowner quotes the proverb, "Blessed are Thou, O Lord . . . who hast not made me a woman."

I try again. "At the well, a man spoke to me of things no one else knows. This man told me everything I have ever done!" I have never felt an ounce of love for any of these people who have always looked down on me. But now I see them thirsting, like me, for something they cannot find in their drink and devilment. With a quick prayer to El Shaddai, the Lord Almighty, I shout, "Come and see! He cannot be the Messiah, can he?"

I am surprised by the number who follow me, and relieved when I see Jesus still at the well. Crowds settle close and listen to the Messiah as darkness falls. One story is of a Samaritan who rescued a Jew even a priest and a Levite had passed by. We beg Jesus to stay in Sychar, and for the next two days our thirst is quenched with grace and forgiveness.

On the morning Jesus departs, men, women, and children see him off. Many tell me it is no longer because of what I said that they believe. "For we have heard for ourselves, and we know that this is truly the Savior of the world."

I cannot imagine never seeing Jesus again, even if I must go alone to Jerusalem.

My thoughts are interrupted by Sarah, one of many who forced me to get water in scorching heat. "Please come to the well with me now?" A dozen other women wait for my answer.

A week ago, I might have used my wit to punish these women for despising me and turning my skin to sunbaked leather. Now I look forward to offering them a drink of water.

Pondering . . .

1.) Ponder the properties and uses of water. Why is "living water" a good metaphor for Jesus, the Spirit, and salvation?

2.) What is your personal testimony of coming to faith in Christ? Have you ever shared your testimony with someone who may not have found Jesus? Ask God to put one person in your path and on your heart so you can share your testimony.

3.) Did the testimony of anyone influence you in your search for salvation, even if you didn't think you were searching? Has anyone's life and faith influenced your own faith? Maybe this Easter season would be a good time to write a thank-you note or take someone to breakfast and talk about her faith-gift.

4.) Are there any people you've given up on—shared your faith and been rejected? Why do you think this person wasn't open to seeking God? Is there anything you can do to help?

Dear God,
Help me share my testimony with
"thirsty" people.

Day 14

MARY OF BETHANY

Hospitality

Cheerfully share your home with those who need a meal or a place to stay.

(1 Peter 4:9, NLT)

Don't hesitate to accept hospitality, because those who work deserve to be fed.

(Matthew 10:10b, NLT)

Do not neglect to show hospitality to strangers, for by doing that some have entertained angels without knowing it.

(Hebrews 13:2)

Then he entered Jerusalem and went into the temple, and when he had looked around at everything, as it was already late, he went out to Bethany with the twelve.

(Mark 11:11)

MARY OF BETHANY
Hospitality

I praise Jehovah Jireh, *The Lord Will Provide*, as I race over sand and stone with fresh fruit from the market. Martha, Lazarus, and I grow our own leeks, onions, mint, cumin, and dill. Yet had I not walked to Jerusalem markets, I would not be carrying honey or pomegranates.

In spite of the heat, I shiver passing the Mount of Olives, where Jesus often prays. Lines of olive groves dance in the breeze. We live on the eastern slope, in Bethany, and Jesus the Messiah will be dining with us this night. For this gift, I could run to the top of the mount and shout my thanks!

• • •

"Honey, Mary?" Martha says, as if I have given her a flock of lambs. She holds up a fat cucumber. "Look what Lazarus brought in from the garden! We will send them with Jesus and his friends. Cucumbers provide a wonderful source of water for travelers."

The aroma of bread from the tabun, our domed clay oven, fills the house. Yesterday I ground barley in the quern until my arms cried out and Lazarus came to my rescue. He shares our love of Jesus and has often accompanied us to hear the Messiah's teachings.

While Martha mashes lentils for her special bean dip, Lazarus sets in place wool-filled mattresses, rolled up until evening. "How many will sleep here tonight?" he shouts.

"I believe Jesus will bring twelve disciples," I shout back. "And nearly as many women who travel with them."

Martha looks up from her task. "Mary, we do not have provisions for that number!"

"We will make do," I assure her. "They are used to sleeping on the ground."

Ignoring me, she shouts to Lazarus, "Place recliners at the men's table. Women should have mats, so lay them in the small room."

Martha's worries threaten to dampen my excitement, so I escape to our garden, where I inhale sage and flowering cucumbers. A memory returns of the first time I heard Jesus speak from the Court of the Gentiles in Jerusalem. His look was of an ordinary man in a common tunic—not of a priest or Sadducee. Since then, I show up whenever he speaks nearby. After seeing him heal Simon the Leper, our neighbor, we were honored to meet Jesus. And now this honor, that Jesus comes to our home!

"Mary!" Martha's cry reaches me from the kitchen. "Someone is coming!"

Pondering . . .

1.) What do you think hospitality means? Where and how do people show hospitality?

2.) Who have been your dinner guests in the past year or two? Why these guests? What do you think they (and you) got out of the visit?

3.) Jesus ended a parable with this advice: "When you give a luncheon or a dinner, do not invite your friends or your brothers or your relatives or rich neighbors, in case they may invite you in return, and you would be repaid. But when you give a banquet, invite the poor, the crippled, the lame, and the blind" (Luke 14:12–13). If you followed this advice and the spirit of it, who would be your next guests?

4.) Do you enjoy preparing for guests, or is it nerve-wracking? Why do you think we get anxious about guests coming? Is there anything you can do to lessen your stress during Easter this year? Is there someone you could invite to church?

Dear God,
Help me show hospitality to guests
for your sake and for theirs.

MARY OF BETHANY

Listening

Now as they went on their way, he entered a certain village where a woman named Martha welcomed him. She had a sister named Mary, who sat at Jesus's feet and listened to what he was saying. But Martha was distracted by her many tasks, so she came to him and asked, "Lord, do you not care that my sister has left me to do all the work by myself? Tell her, then, to help me." But the Lord answered her, "Martha, Martha, you are worried and distracted by many things, but few things are needed—indeed only one. Mary has chosen the better part, which will not be taken away from her."

(Luke 10:38–42)

For he is our God, and we are the people of his pasture and the sheep of his hand. O that today you would listen to his voice!

(Psalm 95:7)

He awakens Me *morning by morning,*
He awakens My ear to listen as a disciple.

(Isaiah 50:4b, NASB)

MARY OF BETHANY
Listening

"It is good to see you again, Mary," Martha says. Magdalene's eyes shine with the truth of her words. "You have met Susanna, who left a business in Jerusalem to join us, and Joanna, wife of Chuza, Herod's steward."

Martha sets a washing bowl on the entry bench. It is an honor to wash the women's feet. Whereas Magdalene's are hardened with calluses, the feet of Susanna and Joanna bleed from open blisters and nettle scratches. "Thank you, Martha," Joanna says. "I have not walked so long as my companions." She smiles at my sister, who sets out the men's wash bowl. "Now, I have come to help."

"How gracious of you!" Martha says. "But you are our guests."

"Mary!" Jesus steps inside, laughing. I yearn to run to him, to catch any falling words from the lips of the Messiah. "I was just telling Matthew and Thomas the story of the seed that fell on hard ground, on rocky soil, thorny soil, and on good soil."

"I have thought much about striving to be good soil, Rabbi. How I long to rid myself of the thorns of worry!" I confess.

Jesus turns to his disciples. "Did I not tell you Mary of Bethany would understand? She has ears to hear."

Martha leads the women to their table, but I have no appetite for food, only for the words of the Messiah. The men recline at table, propped on elbows, leaving one hand free to dip the bread into olive oil. On the recliner next to Jesus, Lazarus is listening to Matthew describe his former life as a tax collector.

I find my spot at Jesus' feet. The men have already said the brachah rishonah: "Blessed are You, Lord our God, King of the Universe." Yet I need more. "Jesus, please teach me to pray."

As if I were the only person in all Israel, Jesus answers me. He speaks about his kingdom to come, not just for Israel, but for Gentiles and foreigners.

Martha runs from table to table, replenishing every bowl. I have heard her sighs but barely noticed her passing until she places a bowl in front of Jesus with a thud that may have cracked her best serving bowl. "Lord, do you not care that my sister has left me to do all the work by myself? Tell her, then, to help me." Murmurs around the table agree with Martha.

Before I can rise to help Martha, Jesus says, "Martha, Martha, you are worried and distracted by many things, but few things are needed—indeed only one. Mary has chosen the better part, which will not be taken away from her."

Tears come as Jesus defends me, for Jesus is the only One I desire to please.

PONDERING . . .

1.) What's your first impression of the two sisters in Bethany? Make a defense for each woman. Are you more of a Martha or a Mary?

2.) How do you "listen" to Jesus? Why does the Apostle John refer to Jesus as the "Word"? *In the beginning was the Word, and the Word was with God, and the Word was God. (John 1:1)*

3.) Do you ever feel put upon unfairly and left to do most of the work? How do you handle it? Anger, controlled resentment, a grudge, or understanding?

4.) Why do you think Jesus "sided with" Mary? What is the "better part" Jesus says Mary chose? How can you be a better "listener" this Easter?

Dear God,
Help me to be a better listener and
to seek to please only you.

Day 16

MARY OF BETHANY

Waiting

Now a certain man was ill, Lazarus of Bethany, the village of Mary and her sister Martha. Mary was the one who anointed the Lord with perfume and wiped his feet with her hair; her brother Lazarus was ill. So the sisters sent a message to Jesus, "Lord, he whom you love is ill." But when Jesus heard it, he said, "This illness does not lead to death; rather, it is for God's glory, so that the Son of God may be glorified through it." Accordingly, though Jesus loved Martha and her sister and Lazarus, after having heard that Lazarus was ill, he stayed two days longer in the place where he was. Then after this he said to the disciples, "Let us go to Judea again." The disciples said to him, "Rabbi, the Jews were just now trying to stone you, and are you going there again?"

(John 11:1–8)

"The Son of Man is to be betrayed into human hands, and they will kill him, and three days after being killed, he will rise again."

(Mark 9:31)

MARY OF BETHANY
Waiting

Gazing out the window from the flickering candlelight of our home to the shining stars above the Mount of Olives, I reflect on the way Jesus' visits have always brought light. I listened to every word when last Jesus came for the Feast of Booths and spent nights in Bethany. He talked to me, not in stories, but in hard words of what is to come.

"Mary?!" Lazarus's call sends me running to his room. I kneel beside his mattress and brush sweat-slicked hair from his face. The odor of his illness surrounds my brother.

"Water . . . please?" The words have to climb over parched lips.

Before I can rise, Martha rushes in with a cold cloth and fresh bowl of water. He takes one sip, and a fit of coughing overcomes him. "Mary, our brother worsens by the hour."

I want Jesus. We hear of his miracles east of the Jordan. Only his presence can bring healing and peace. "I must go and find Jesus." Yet leaving my brother would wrench my soul.

Martha shakes her head. "You are known to the priests, who would arrest you for your devotion to Jesus. Besides, I need you here. I am weakened from lack of sleep."

Lazarus groans, and my desperation grows. "We must get word to Jesus! He heals strangers and Gentiles. He will surely heal his beloved friend!"

"I will ask Simon the Leper to deliver our message," Martha says. Simon, now healed by Jesus, shares our courtyard and cooker. He also shares our love of Jesus.

In minutes, Martha returns. "Simon says he is honored to help. He will leave immediately."

Days pass, and Lazarus slips into a sleep from which we cannot awaken him. When Simon returns, I race barefooted across sand, straining to see behind him. "Simon, where is Jesus?"

"He remains in Galilee," Simon says, his voice dry as sand.

Martha and I watch Lazarus's breath diminish until there is no more. Our brother dies.

Our house fills with mourners, many who believe that the spirit departs on the third day. On the fourth day, when the hope of Lazarus's lingering spirit is gone, I sit amidst wailing mourners while Martha wraps linen and spices around the body as if to hold it together.

I watch as my brother is placed on the stone ledge inside our family's cave. Only when the stone is rolled against the opening do I cry out from deep inside, where I do not recognize myself. I accept no words of consolation, for there is only One whose words I desire to hear.

Pondering . . .

1.) Have you waited desperately for something or someone? Why do you think you had to wait?

2.) If you've had to wait for a long time, did you lose hope? How can we learn to wait with hope, no matter the outcome?

3.) What good can come from waiting? Do you know anyone who's waiting in desperation? How could you help?

4.) How does the presence of Christ help while you wait? Is there someone you might comfort by a visit or a phone call this Easter?

Dear God,
I praise you and thank you for
your love and wisdom
when I have to wait on you.

Day 17

MARTHA

Life

When Martha heard that Jesus was coming, she went and met him, while Mary stayed at home. Martha said to Jesus, "Lord, if you had been here, my brother would not have died. But even now I know that God will give you whatever you ask of him." Jesus said to her, "Your brother will rise again."

(John 11:20–23)

When he had said this, he cried with a loud voice, "Lazarus, come out!" The dead man came out, his hands and feet bound with strips of cloth and his face wrapped in a cloth. Jesus said to them, "Unbind him, and let him go."

(John 11:43–44)

"I am the Resurrection and the life. Those who believe in me, even though they die, will live, and everyone who lives and believes in me will never die."

(John 11:25–26)

MARTHA
Life

Lazarus has been gone four days. How I miss my brother's laughter, his stories, his manner with older women and young children. Mary barely eats and fails to greet our guests.

Simon interrupts my sadness and motions me to the courtyard. "Jesus is coming."

Without thought to my guests or our traditions that Mary and I must stay at home for seven days, I break into a run. Jesus is coming. When we meet, I say to him my constant thought. "Lord, if you had been here, my brother would not have died. But even now I know that God will give you whatever you ask."

Jesus stares into my eyes with a profound love. "Martha, Lazarus will rise again."

It is not the answer I have hoped for. "I know that he will rise again on the last day."

Jesus answers me in the way I have seen him speak to Mary. "I am the Resurrection and the Life. Those who believe in me, even though they die will live, and everyone who lives and believes in me will never die. Do you believe this?"

I am not certain I understand as would my sister. "I believe that you are the Messiah, the Son of God, the One bringing salvation to the world."

"Please tell your sister I will wait here to see her."

I hurry back to Mary and whisper, "The Teacher is here and is calling for you."

Mary races with me to the village edge, mourners trailing behind. She kneels at Jesus' feet, weeping. "Lord, if you had been here, my brother would not have died."

Jesus weeps with Mary, the only time I have seen his tears. "Show me where you have laid him." When we arrive at the burial cave, he commands, "Take away the stone."

He must know that no one enters the tomb for a year, when decomposition frees the bones to be placed in a container and laid into the cave wall's slot. All my spices will not delay decomposition. "Lord, already there is a stench, for he has been dead four days."

"Martha, did I not tell you that if you believed, you would see the glory of God?"

I nod to the men to remove the stone. Then Jesus shouts, "Lazarus, come out!"

Some in the crowd muffle laughter; others cover their mouths or eyes. Mary no longer weeps. A shuffling issues from the tomb, and out hobbles Lazarus, bound with strips of my cloth. Jesus commands, "Unbind him, and let him go," an order Mary and I gratefully obey.

Lazarus looks better than he has for months. His voice is raspy but filled with praise.

Several Pharisees remain at the back of the onlookers, whispering furiously, then heading toward Jerusalem as if escaping a sandstorm. They do not appear to share in our joy.

PONDERING . . .

1.) When Jesus received word of Lazarus's illness, he chose not to go right away to Bethany. Have you ever had to wait for help—a doctor, a friend—while you or a loved one grew worse? Ponder how Mary and Martha may have felt.

2.) Why do you think Jesus stayed where he was instead of going straight to Lazarus? Ponder what Jesus said about the illness being for God's glory so that the Son of God would be glorified through it.

3.) In the Eastern tradition, many mourners were expected to grieve openly and loudly. Sometimes mourners were hired to express emotions of grief. If you've lost a loved one, what actions from friends and family were the most helpful or comforting?

4.) What exactly do you think of Jesus' claim: "I am the Resurrection and the Life"? How would you explain those words to a nonbeliever? Do you believe that you will never die?

Dear God,
Thank you for the security of knowing
I'll be with you for eternity!

SALOME

Ambition

Then Peter said in reply, "Look, we have left everything and followed you. What then will we have?" Jesus said to them, "Truly I tell you, at the renewal of all things, when the Son of Man is seated on the throne of his glory, you who have followed me will also sit on twelve thrones, judging the twelve tribes of Israel. And everyone who has left houses or brothers or sisters or father or mother or wife or children or fields for my name's sake will receive a hundredfold and will inherit eternal life. But many who are first will be last, and the last will be first."

(Matthew 19:27–30)

"And do you seek great things for yourself?

Do not seek them. . . ."

(Jeremiah 45:5, NKJV)

SALOME
Ambition

On our journey I have enjoyed the company of Joanna, wife of Chuza, and of Peter's wife. Both understand the difficulties balancing marriage and ministry. Though Zebedee shares our mission, without James and John to bring in fish, he depends on the hired men of Capernaum, who are not always dependable. Still, I know God has big plans for us to be here with Jesus.

Tonight, Joanna and I sit apart from the others, though close enough to the fires to ward off the night's chill. "Salome, did you ever imagine you would witness so many miracles?"

"No," I confide. "Though I suppose I have always anticipated such an experience." It has been a long day of helping desperate people from all over Galilee. We try to keep them in some kind of order, but a few shove to be first in line.

Joanna glances to the men behind us. "James and John seem especially close to Jesus."

"They are!" I answer, perhaps too fast. Talk of the thrones in Jesus' kingdom has given me ideas. "My boys were with Jesus when he healed the daughter of Jairus. Jesus allowed no one into the room except my boys . . . and Peter."

"I see." Joanna yawns and gets to her feet. "I must sleep. Are you coming?"

I am not coming. I am thinking. "Later. Goodnight, Joanna."

I find my boys, James filling a row of lanterns while John writes on his papyri. "Boys, join me for a little walk before I retire." They exchange the look I used to receive when I informed them that studying the Torah must come before playing pebble games. Once we are alone, I sit on a boulder where Jesus often prays. "You know Jesus favors you, do you not?"

John elbows his brother. "See? I told you."

"Tomorrow I plan to ask Jesus if you two can sit on his right and left in his kingdom."

John's face takes on the eagerness of his childhood. "Yes!"

"Let's ask before anyone else tries!" James turns as if he's ready to burst into Jesus' tent right now.

I put out an arm to prevent him. "Get a good night's sleep. We will go together to see Jesus tomorrow."

PONDERING . . .

1.) How would you define "ambition"? Is ambition a good thing or a bad thing? Explain.

2.) Do you think of yourself as ambitious? Would others see you that way? Have your drive and ambition ever created conflict and competition?

3.) Have you ever lacked ambition? Explain what you might have done if you'd followed through with your secret ambitions? How could Easter refine your motivations to achieve?

4.) What do you want to achieve more than anything else, and what are you doing to get there? How can you know if your ambition fits into God's ambition, or plans, for you?

Dear God,
Help me to find a balance between
wanting too much and giving up too soon.

SALOME

Misplaced Boldness

While Jesus was going up to Jerusalem, he took the twelve disciples aside by themselves and said to them, "Look, we are going up to Jerusalem, and the Son of Man will be handed over to the chief priests and scribes, and they will condemn him to death; then they will hand him over to the gentiles to be mocked and flogged and crucified, and on the third day he will be raised."

(Matthew 20:17–19)

Then the mother of the sons of Zebedee came to him with her sons, and kneeling before him, she asked a favor of him. And he said to her, "What do you want?" She said to him, "Declare that these two sons of mine will sit, one at your right hand and one at your left, in your kingdom."

(Matthew 20:20–21)

Do nothing from selfish ambition or empty conceit, but in humility regard others as better than yourselves.

(Philippians 2:3)

But if you have bitter envy and selfish ambition in your hearts, do not be arrogant and lie about the truth.

(James 3:14)

SALOME
Misplaced Boldness

Such a crowd follows us to Jerusalem that I cannot reach Jesus to ask my favor. He continues to heal one by one, touching even the lepers, answering the foolish questions of the Pharisees.

On our approach to Jerusalem, the crowd separates, and I pull aside my boys from Jesus' teaching. I barely hear Jesus' words, though Magdalene, Susanna, and Joanna seem upset. I will talk to them later, but now I must fulfill my mission. "Boys, are you ready?" They nod with vigor.

Before Jesus can rejoin the crowd, I rush to him and kneel. "Jesus, I have a favor to ask."

Jesus smiles at me, his head tilted. "What is it you want, Salome?"

"Declare that these two sons of mine can sit on your right and left in your kingdom."

A sadness overshadows him. "Are you able to drink the cup I am about to drink?"

I am uncertain of his meaning, but James and John answer as one. "We are able!"

"You will indeed drink my cup," Jesus says, "but seats in the kingdom have been prepared by my Father."

Astonished and fighting anger, I walk back to Joanna and Magdalene. "I do not understand him! Why would he ask if James and John are able to drink the cup, whatever that is." I smooth my hair and nearly burn my palm, so hot is the sun.

Magdalene lays a hand on my shoulder. "Did you not hear what Jesus told us?" I shrug. It was something about Jerusalem. "He said that in Jerusalem, he would be betrayed and condemned to death, mocked, flogged, . . . and crucified."

Joanna adds, "Salome, that is the cup you asked for your boys!" She storms away before I can make sense of her words, of Jesus' words. I turn to Magdalene, whose eyes flood with tears. She shakes her head and runs after Joanna.

I look back at James and John and see them surrounded by angry disciples: "I am the one he calls 'Rock!'" Peter shouts. "I was first to believe in him!" Andrew counters. I cannot make out the sharp words of the others.

Jesus calls everyone to him and motions them to sit on the ground. "Whoever wishes to be great must be your servant. In my Father's kingdom, the last shall be first, and the first last."

He turns his sad smile to me, but I cannot look him in the eyes. I know what he must think of me.

I cannot be here. I cannot stay here. Wrapping my shawl around me, I leave everything else and run, starting my long journey back to Capernaum and to Zebedee, who will no doubt share in my everlasting shame.

I am never coming back.

Pondering . . .

1.) Has your attempt at helping someone ever backfired, hurting or embarrassing them? What do you think your motives were?

2.) How do you handle a situation when you realize you were wrong? Fight or flight? Why do you think it's so hard to admit when we're wrong?

3.) Ponder what you think Jesus meant by the last will be first and the first last. In most cases, which one are you, first or last?

4.) The apostle Paul wrote Timothy: The sins of some people are conspicuous and precede them to judgment, while the sins of others follow them there (1 Timothy 5:24). Do you think your sins are conspicuous, or secretly destined to follow you to judgment?

Dear God,
Help me see my sin clearly
and not try to hide it.
Thank you for forgiving me.

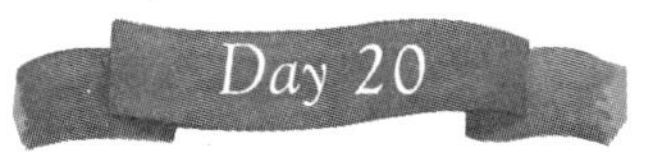

Day 20

JOANNA, WIFE OF CHUZA

Triumph

Then they brought it [the colt] to Jesus, and after throwing their cloaks on the colt, they set Jesus on it. . . . Now as he was approaching the path down from the Mount of Olives, the whole multitude of the disciples began to praise God joyfully with a loud voice for all the deeds of power that they had seen, saying, "Blessed is the king who comes in the name of the Lord! Peace in heaven, and glory in the highest heaven!" Some of the Pharisees in the crowd said to him, "Teacher, order your disciples to stop." He answered, "I tell you, if these were silent, the stones would shout out."

(Luke 19:35–40)

Rejoice greatly, O daughter Zion! Shout aloud, O daughter Jerusalem! See, your king comes to you; triumphant and victorious is he, humble and riding on a donkey, on a colt, the foal of a donkey.

(Zechariah 9:9)

JOANNA, WIFE OF CHUZA
Triumph

I have chosen to remain in Jerusalem to celebrate Passover with Chuza while Jesus and the others make their way from Capernaum. Since Lazarus was raised from the dead, Jesus and Lazarus are hated by religious leaders. I have warned Jesus not to come. Thousands from all parts of the world crush onto Temple grounds in hope of seeing the Healer.

I press through the crowd and am assaulted by strange smoke, perfumes, and sweat mingled with the stench of slaughtered sacrifices. I am swept along and through the East Gate, where prophecy says the Messiah will enter. Outside the wall, Jews and Gentiles line the road, many waving palm branches ripped from trees. I fear I will not see Jesus before I am trampled.

Then I see him, in the tunic his mother made for him, riding on the back of a donkey. Shouts echo: "Praise God!" "Hosanna!" "The King is coming!" "Blessed is he who comes in the name of the Lord!" Others shout "Hallelujah!" as a war cry: "Save us now!"

What will happen when they learn Jesus is not here to overthrow Rome?

As Jesus nears, I see Philip and Thomas and the other Mary, who look rapt with joy and pride, as if this victory is what we, too, have waited for. It is wonderful to see Jesus praised and recognized as the King of Kings. Pharisees in the crowd display anger and defeat. So perhaps it is I who am mistaken. Why could not Jesus set up his kingdom here and now?

But as Jesus rides past me, greeting the children, his eyes meet mine, and I see the depth of his sorrow. He knows what lies in the hearts of every one of us, and still his love is great.

After a time, the crowd disperses, leaving Pharisees to question Jesus. He is harsh with them, denouncing scribes and Pharisees, calling them whitewashed tombs, blind guides, and hypocrites.

That evening I report everything to Chuza. "Jesus told them that when he is lifted up on the cross, he will draw everyone to himself. Surely, he cannot mean the cross of crucifixion. His Father would never choose such a horror for his Son."

Chuza sits next to me. "And yet, did not El Shaddai command Abraham to sacrifice his son?"

I am quick to answer. "And El Shaddai, the source of all blessings, provided another sacrifice at the last moment, freeing Isaac to his father." *El Shaddai, this is my prayer.*

PONDERING . . .

1.) How have you pictured Palm Sunday, the Triumphal Entry? Consider the feelings Jesus may have had entering Jerusalem, knowing what would follow.

2.) Has there been a time when you, like Joanna, saw things clearly, but utterly opposite from those around you? Did you alter your opinion in any way? Why or why not?

3.) Imagine you were in the palm-waving crowd seeing Jesus on a donkey and coming your way. What thoughts might have gone through your head? This Easter, try to imagine yourself as a bystander or as one of the women journeying with Jesus. Ponder what this real, live person may have been feeling.

4.) Easter is all about Christ's sacrifice. Have you ever done a sacrificial act? Taking the blame so someone wouldn't get into worse trouble? Giving more than you needed to?

Dear God,
Thank you for being my King
and providing my Sacrifice.
Purify my heart as I celebrate Easter.

MARY OF BETHANY

Devotion

Six days before the Passover Jesus came to Bethany, the home of Lazarus, whom he had raised from the dead. There they gave a dinner for him. Martha served, and Lazarus was one of those reclining with him. Mary took a pound of costly perfume made of pure nard, anointed Jesus's feet, and wiped them with her hair. The house was filled with the fragrance of the perfume. But Judas Iscariot, one of his disciples (the one who was about to betray him), said, "Why was this perfume not sold for three hundred denarii and the money given to the poor?" (He said this not because he cared about the poor but because he was a thief; he kept the common purse and used to steal what was put into it.)

(John 12:1–6)

Am I now seeking human approval or God's approval? Or am I trying to please people? If I were still pleasing people, I would not be a servant of Christ.

(Galatians 1:10)

For if we are beside ourselves, it is for God; if we are in our right mind, it is for you.

(2 Corinthians 5:13)

MARY OF BETHANY
Devotion

Tonight, Jesus and his followers will dine with us in the home of Simon the Leper, who shares our courtyard. As soon as Jesus arrives, stories sweep around the table like sycamore leaves in autumn.

Lazarus reclines beside Jesus and pours aromatic wine. Peter speaks above the others. "Not one, but two blind beggars shouted by the road. Of course, Jesus cured them, a two-for-one miracle!" He laughs so loud that his wife nudges his shoulder.

I look toward the door, still hoping to see Joanna and Salome, who usually help with dinners. "Is Salome coming?" I ask James.

James glances to John, then says, "Mother has not journeyed with us for some time."

From my place at the feet of my Savior, I sense a heaviness from my Lord. I believe I understand, and my heart aches. I rise, knowing what I must do.

On my dresser is my only valuable possession, an alabaster jar of pure nard from North India and worth a year of Lazarus' wages. Father intended it for my dowry, and I have imagined using the money to build a home and a family of my own. But Elohim has higher plans.

I see no surprise on my Master's face when I return. The room whispers as I kneel at the feet of Jesus. The round, marbled vessel has a long, thin neck and is nearly as precious as its contents. It takes all my strength to break the neck of the jar. Instantly, the sweet aroma blankets all conversation. Have I ever experienced truer worship from my heart?

Beginning at Jesus' feet, I let the thick oil cover his blistered toes. I uncover my head and remove the combs that I may dry the excess oil with my hair. This brings gasps from those watching, for tradition teaches that a moral woman never lets her hair down in public. Caring only what Jesus thinks, I pour the rest of the oil over his head, and I am dizzy with the aroma of anointing the Son of God.

Judas Iscariot pounds the table, spilling wine. "That perfume could have been sold for 300 denarii and given to the poor! She's wasting it!"

Murmurs of agreement come from all sides. I sit again at the feet of Jesus. His hand rests on my head. "Leave her alone! She has kept this gift for the day of my burial. Mary's loving act will be spoken of forever."

My heart warms with Jesus' defense of me . . . again. I am honored and grateful, though my soul is beyond sorrowful that the time of my Lord's burial is upon us.

PONDERING . . .

1.) Have you ever been accused of bad motives when you honestly meant well? Did anyone speak up for you? Have you ever spoken up for someone who has been falsely accused?

2.) What is the most sacrificial gift you have ever given? Why did you give it? Did you have "giver's remorse" later? In this Easter season, is there something God may be nudging you to do, or give, sacrificially?

3.) Do you ever sense God's approval when everyone else seems to disapprove? Explain.

4.) Jesus watched people drop money into the Temple treasury in Jerusalem—some a great deal of money; others, like a poor widow, only two pennies (Mark 12:41–44). Jesus told his disciples the widow put in more than all the others. Ponder what he meant and what his message means to you.

Dear God,
Show me how to love you
and truly worship you
as Mary of Bethany did.

THREE RELIGIOUS TRIALS

First Religious Trial: Annas

So the soldiers, their officer, and the Jewish police arrested Jesus and bound him. First they took him to Annas, who was the father-in-law of Caiaphas, the high priest that year. Caiaphas was the one who had advised the Jews that it was better to have one person die for the people.

(John 18:12–14)

Then the high priest questioned Jesus about his disciples and about his teaching. Jesus answered, "I have spoken openly to the world; I have always taught in synagogues and in the temple, where all the Jews come together. I have said nothing in secret. Why do you ask me? Ask those who heard what I said to them; they know what I said." When he had said this, one of the police standing nearby struck Jesus on the face, saying, "Is that how you answer the high priest?" Jesus answered, "If I have spoken wrongly, testify to the wrong. But if I have spoken rightly, why do you strike me?"

(John 18:19–23)

Second Religious Trial: Caiaphas

Then Annas sent him bound to Caiaphas the high priest.

(John 18:24)

Now the chief priests and the whole council were looking for false testimony against Jesus so that they might put him to death, but they found none, though many false witnesses came forward. . . .

(Matthew 26:59–60)

But Jesus was silent. Then the high priest said to him, "I put you under oath before the living God, tell us if you are the Messiah, the Son of God." Jesus said to him, "You have said so. But I tell you, From now on you will see the Son of Man seated at the right hand of Power and coming on the clouds of heaven."

Then the high priest tore his clothes and said, "He has blasphemed! Why do we still need witnesses? You have now heard his blasphemy. What do you think?" They answered, "He deserves death." Then they spat in his face and struck him, and some slapped him, saying, "Prophesy to us, you Messiah! Who is it that struck you?"

(Matthew 26:63–68)

Third Religious Trial: Sanhedrin

When day came, the assembly of the elders of the people, both chief priests and scribes, gathered together, and they brought him to their council. They said, "If you are the Messiah, tell us." He replied, "If I tell you, you will not believe, and if I question you, you will not answer. But from now on the Son of Man will be seated at the right hand of the power of God." All of them asked, "Are you, then, the Son of God?" He said to them, "You say that I am." Then they said, "What further testimony do we need? We have heard it ourselves from his own lips!"

(Luke 22:66–71)

Day 22

JOANNA, WIFE OF CHUZA

Betrayed

Each day of Passover week increases the ire of the Pharisees and Sadducees. Nicodemus and a few other secret followers of Jesus keep their silence while he exposes the hypocrisy of the religious leaders with parables and harsh words. He has cleansed the Temple again, taught crowds who hail him as the Messiah, then returned to Bethany with us each night.

This night, however, Jesus will break bread with the twelve in a Jerusalem Upper Room, while Martha hosts the women. I will not join them; Chuza has made plans. Rumors of Jesus' imminent arrest travel through the palace like a two-headed snake. The city is on high alert, with Roman soldiers and Jewish guards demanding to know Jesus' whereabouts.

I ready for bed, worn from frivolous talk with those I once thought friends. Sleep does not come. Suddenly, I hear the stomping of boots. I race to the window and look down at fully armed soldiers. My first thought is that we are at war. Then an even worse truth: "They have found him, Chuza!"

We dress and rush outside to be enveloped by a mob of soldiers. Chuza asks a young servant who often dines with him, "What is happening?"

"Jesus has been arrested. One of his closest followers betrayed him!"

"No!" This cannot be true. We love Jesus and owe him our very lives.

Around us, others repeat their rumors: "Temple guards arrested him in Gethsemane, though who knows why he would go there in the middle of the night?"

I know. The Garden of Gethsemane is one place Jesus goes to pray. The betrayal is real and burns in my throat. Chuza urges me to return to the palace, but I start for Gethsemane when I hear a ruckus from the city gate and recognize several of the disciples running across the square.

Moments later, bound and surrounded by more guards than I can count—Jesus is dragged into the City of David. "Where are they going?" I demand of no one, everyone.

A bone-thin, ageless man answers, "To Annas, to Caiaphas, and to the Sanhedrin, where Jesus will rightly be sentenced to death. He has deceived the nation and deserves death."

"They can't sentence anyone to death!" I protest. This is true as Rome forbids it.

The man leans in and breathes garlic and ale into my face. "Then they will take him to Pilate, the Governor. *He* can execute anyone he pleases."

PONDERING . . .

1.) Do you now, or have you ever, had an "enemy," or a person or group you avoided because you felt they didn't accept you? Jesus forgave his enemies—have you been able to do the same?

2.) Judas had journeyed with the disciples, joining in the camaraderie, seeing miracle after miracle. Jesus called him, loved him. How do you think Jesus felt when Judas betrayed him with a kiss? Have you ever been betrayed? Describe how that felt—feels.

3.) What are ways we may subtly deny Christ? Ponder how this Easter could be different, and ask God to help you talk openly about Jesus and what Easter really means.

4.) Joanna saw the crowds transform from praise at the Triumphal Entry to shouts of hate and condemnation. Why do you think so many turned on Jesus? Has anything sad or disappointing ever affected the way you look at Jesus?

Dear God,
Please help me to be loyal and trustworthy.

Day 23

MARY MAGDALENE

Empathy

Joanna arrived when the waxing moon lit the black sky brighter than Martha's lantern. We huddle on Martha's sleeping porch, tightening our circle with every word from Joanna. My mind forms dreadful images as she unfolds the nightmare—Jesus arrested, dragged, beaten, mocked before Annas, the old chief priest, and then to Caiaphas, both priests appointed by Rome, of course.

Joanna speaks so fast I cannot keep up. "Three Jewish trials all falsely found Jesus guilty," she summarizes.

"Three? And he was betrayed?" My head throbs as if I, too, have been beaten.

"We don't know who betrayed Jesus," Joanna says, "but Peter denied knowing him."

"Peter would not betray Jesus!" Quiet Susanna surprises me with her loud assertion, though I agree with her. My guess would be Judas, bribed by silver coins.

Joanna continues as if forced to release the knowledge she holds. "In the Sanhedrin, Sadducees told lies, though no two witnesses could agree. Still, they convicted Jesus by acclamation, condemning him for blasphemy, for claiming to be the Son of God."

"Which he is!" cries Mary, mother of James and Joses. "They break their own rules by holding a trial during feast time, at night, without counsel. Each member should vote individually. Nicodemus, Josephus, and others may have dissented.

"The Sanhedrin sentenced Jesus to death." Joanna looks away, and silence descends.

"A death sentence means nothing since they have no such authority!" I insist.

I see on Martha's face that I have given her hope. "Then is it over? Did they release him?"

Joanna takes her time to answer. "They were sending him to Pilate when I left to come here." The other Mary breaks into tears. Joanna hugs her and presses on. "Yes, we know the governor is a violent man, but I am familiar with his wife. She knows about Jesus, and I have heard that she suffered in a dream and fears her husband's mistreatment of an innocent man." This is what we all want to believe, but the hope dangles in thickening air. We all know the Romans love crucifixions.

Martha's sister, Mary, has not spoken, nor did she show surprise at Joanna's news. When she now speaks, I strain to hear. "If Pilate ignores his wife's warning, Jesus, the only guiltless man to have lived on earth, will be sentenced to death on a cross."

PONDERING . . .

1.) Magdalene had deep empathy for Jesus. How would you define "empathy"? Are there people who could use your empathy this Easter?

2.) Do you believe that Jesus was the only one to live on earth without sin? How can you know for sure? What could you offer to someone who doesn't believe this?

3.) Why do you think the religious leaders were so intent on convicting and killing Jesus? What do you think you'd do to stop them?

4.) If friends or acquaintances verbally accuse someone behind that person's back, do you keep quiet? Laugh along? Stand up for the person, even if not a friend?

Dear God,
Please help me to empathize
and try to understand others.

THREE ROMAN POLITICAL TRIALS

First Roman Trial: Pilate

When morning came, all the chief priests and the elders of the people conferred together against Jesus in order to bring about his death. They bound him, led him away, and handed him over to Pilate the governor.

(Matthew 27:1–2)

Then Pilate asked him [Jesus], "Are you the king of the Jews?" He answered, "You say so." Then Pilate said to the chief priests and the crowds, "I find no basis for an accusation against this man." But they were insistent and said, "He stirs up the people by teaching throughout all Judea, from Galilee where he began even to this place."

(Luke 23:3–5)

Second Roman Trial: Herod

And when he [Pilate] learned that he [Jesus] was under Herod's jurisdiction, he sent him off to Herod, who was himself in Jerusalem at that time. When Herod saw Jesus, he was very glad, for he had been wanting to see him for a long time because he had heard about him and was hoping to see him perform some sign. He questioned him at some length, but Jesus gave him no answer. The chief priests and the scribes stood by vehemently accusing him. Even Herod with his soldiers treated him with contempt and mocked him; then he put an elegant robe on him and sent him back to Pilate. That same day Herod and Pilate became friends with each other; before this they had been enemies.

(Luke 23:7–12)

Third Roman Trial: Pilate … and the People

While he [Pilate] was sitting on the judgment seat, his wife sent word to him, "Have nothing to do with that innocent man, for today I have suffered a great deal because of a dream about him."

(Matthew 27:19)

Pilate then called together the chief priests, the leaders, and the people and said to them, "You brought me this man as one who was inciting the people, and here I have examined him in your presence and have not found this man guilty of any of your charges against him. Neither has Herod, for he sent him back to us. Indeed, he has done nothing to deserve death. I will therefore have him flogged and release him."

(Luke 23:13–16)

So when Pilate saw that he could do nothing but rather that a riot was beginning, he took some water and washed his hands before the crowd, saying, "I am innocent of this man's blood; see to it yourselves."

(Matthew 27:24)

Day 24

MARY MAGDALENE

Injustice

I am first to run from Martha's home to Jerusalem. I make so much noise stumbling and wheezing that I don't bother praying quietly, but in cries that should reach heaven. Long before I enter the city, I hear shouts of "Crucify! Crucify!" Only days ago, they shouted praise.

Sunrise cannot be distant when I see Mary, wife of Clopas, her hair wrapped in a rag scarf. She is pressed by crowds in the courtyard of Pilate's Palace Praetorium. "Mary!"

She runs to embrace me. "Oh, Magdalene! There is no justice, only cruelty." I nod for her to tell me. "Jesus arrived badly beaten at Pilate's palace. They spoke, and the governor could find nothing wrong in him." A spark of hope that rises in me extinguishes as Mary continues. "When Pilate realized Jesus was under Herod's jurisdiction, he sent Jesus to Herod, who wished to see miracles. Jesus would not do as Herod wanted, so even though Herod found nothing to condemn, he sent Jesus back to Pilate. Yet before ridding himself of the Messiah, Herod had soldiers mock and beat and—." She breaks off in tears.

I look to the elevated platform, where horrific cruelty is on display in the battered body of my Lord, in purple bruising and streaks of blood obscuring his face. Jesus, still the embodiment of peace, lovingkindness, and truth, stands next to Pilate, who sits in the bema, the judgment seat. Shouts of "Crucify! Crucify!" grow more threatening.

Finally, Pilate speaks. "Neither Herod nor I see any guilt in this man. I will have him flogged and released."

My knees buckle at the thought of a Roman flogging; for while a Jewish flogging must stop at 39 lashes, one shy of a death sentence, Roman floggings continue until the soldier tires. Their leather flagellum whips are embedded with pieces of bone and iron, or metal spikes at the end, designed not to lash as do Jewish whips, but to slash, exposing sinews and bone.

Mary Clopas turns away when Jesus is dragged back to the tribunal, but I cannot look away from exposed ribs, muscles, and inner workings that should be enfleshed. Pilate exchanges words with Jesus, though I cannot hear.

Then Pilate addresses us. "Shall I not free your king?"

The religious leaders have stirred the crowd, and all around are raised fists. "Crucify him!" "We have no king but Caesar!"

Pilate washes his hands as if innocent, then sends the true King of Kings to be crucified.

PONDERING . . .

1.) Matthew reports that Pilate's wife sent her husband a message warning him to leave Jesus, the innocent man, alone. When have you ignored a warning or piece of advice, then faced the consequences?

2.) In the end, Pilate went along with the crowd and sent Jesus to be crucified. Have you ever gone along with the crowd, then regretted it? Ponder what you might do this Easter to please only Christ, even though others might tease or object.

3.) Groups of people can lead to disaster and a mob mentality. But groups can also be a force for good. What good could you do with a group of Christian brothers and sisters this Easter season, something you wouldn't be "brave" enough to do on your own?

4.) Ponder what you think qualifies as an "injustice." Recall incidents of injustice reported in the news. When have you been guilty, even in your thoughts, of injustice?

Dear God,
Please make me sensitive to
injustice in the world and in my heart.

Day 25

MARY MAGDALENE

Sorrow

So Pilate released Barabbas to them. He ordered Jesus flogged with a lead-tipped whip, then turned him over to the Roman soldiers to be crucified. Some of the governor's soldiers took Jesus into their headquarters and called out the entire regiment. They stripped him and put a scarlet robe on him. They wove thorn branches into a crown and put it on his head, and they placed a reed stick in his right hand as a scepter. Then they knelt before him in mockery and taunted, "Hail! King of the Jews!" And they spit on him and grabbed the stick and struck him on the head with it. When they were finally tired of mocking him, they took off the robe and put his own clothes on him again.

Then they led him away to be crucified.

(Matthew 27:26–31, NLT)

He was despised and rejected by men; a man of sorrows, and acquainted with grief; and as one from whom men hide their faces he was despised, and we esteemed him not.

(Isaiah 53:3, RSV)

But he was pierced for our rebellion, crushed for our sins. He was beaten so we could be whole. He was whipped so we could be healed.

(Isaiah 53:5, NLT)

MARY MAGDALENE
Sorrow

Mary, wife of Clopas, and I part—she to find the mother of Jesus, I to find and follow Jesus. I ache to think of kind and gentle Mary. How she must suffer with her son!

A Roman cohort of hundreds surrounds Jesus and the crowd following. I join in as they pass through the Gennath, the Garden Gate, and outside the western wall. Jesus stumbles under the weight of the crossbar and receives kicks as he heaves the heavy patibulum across his shoulders like a yoke. A few steps and he is overcome again, for he is weak from blood loss and brutality. I try to push closer, where I could help bear the weight. I would fight to do so.

A Roman captain on horseback forces a pilgrim from North Africa to carry the cross and not slow the Crucifixion. I am grateful to this Passover visitor they call Simon from Cyrene.

Many women of Jerusalem whose lives have been changed by Jesus line the winding path, as do women who traveled with us from Galilee. Soldiers take the long, public route as an added humiliation, through the rancid meat markets and public squares, where noxious perfumes sting eyes and throat. And everywhere is the stench of thousands of animal sacrifices.

At one point the women of Jerusalem gather for the passing Messiah. When he arrives, their weeping grows more desperate. I feel what they feel and love how deeply they love. They are the ones who prepare wine mixed with gall and myrrh to lessen the pain of crucifixion.

Jesus turns to them: "Daughters of Jerusalem, do not weep for me, but weep for yourselves and your children." One soldier kicks him as a second shoves his head to keep going. If I could, I would kick both of them until they are the ones weeping.

We reach Golgotha, the Place of the Skull, named for its shape . . . or from many skulls beneath the dirt. I have lost sight of Jesus until I see soldiers offer him the calming wine. I pray it gives him relief. When the drink touches his lips, Jesus pulls back and refuses it.

A mounted soldier next to me sighs. "He will regret that. The drink is bitter but would be worth bitterness to be sedated."

I try to reach Jesus to make him drink the potion and lessen his pain. Only when I see the calm on his face, I stop. And I understand. My Savior refuses to lessen his pain because he is paying for my sin. The cost to redeem us all is high and will not come at a bargain.

PONDERING . . .

1.) How would you explain the difference between sadness and sorrow? So far this Easter season, are you feeling either one? How can Jesus help?

2.) The apostle Paul described two types of sorrow in his letter to believers in Corinth: *Godly sorrow brings repentance that leads to salvation and leaves no regret, but worldly sorrow brings death* (2 Corinthians 7:10, NIV). Ponder the different types of sorrow in your own life.

3.) How would you define "regret." Are there any regrets hanging over you right now? What might you do to deal with regret or guilt feelings?

4.) Can you think of a time when you felt deep sorrow for a friend? For someone you barely knew? For people you've never known and probably never will? What kinds of things would you imagine break God's heart? Do you share any of those heartaches?

Dear God,
Lord, thank you for your compassion.
Break my heart with the things
and people that break yours.

Day 26

MARY, MOTHER OF JESUS

Agony

There they crucified him and with him two others, one on either side, with Jesus between them. Pilate also had an inscription written and put on the cross. It read, "Jesus of Nazareth, the King of the Jews." Many of the Jews read this inscription, because the place where Jesus was crucified was near the city; and it was written in Hebrew, in Latin, and in Greek. Then the chief priests of the Jews said to Pilate, "Do not write, 'The King of the Jews,' but, 'This man said, I am King of the Jews.'" Pilate answered, "What I have written I have written."

(John 19:18 22)

*By a perversion of justice he was taken away.
Who could have imagined his future? For he was
cut off from the land of the living, stricken for the
transgression of my people. They made his grave
with the wicked and his tomb with the rich, although
he had done no violence, and there was
no deceit in his mouth.*

(Isaiah 53:8–9)

*Dogs surround me, a pack of villains encircles me;
they pierce my hands and my feet.*

(Psalm 22:16, NIV)

MARY, MOTHER OF JESUS
Agony

I have feared this moment since the birth of Jesus, my son. Each year Joseph and I awaited the Day of Atonement, instituted by God to pay for our sins. One goat was sacrificed, and the other set loose, carrying our sins into the wilderness. Did we allow our hearts to realize that this ancient ritual was a picture of what now unfolds before me?

I cannot lift my gaze to see. Not yet.

I am grateful for John's hand on my arm as we press through angry crowds to be closer to the cross—to my son. I insisted on coming here, with or without John. Mary, wife of Clopas, follows behind me, and I draw on her quiet strength. I see the sign posted to explain—in Greek, Latin, and Hebrew—the crimes that led to the cruel execution. Pilate has had it inscribed: Jesus of Nazareth, the King of the Jews. The words are perhaps the only truth to come from Emperor Tiberius' puppet governor.

I can no longer keep my gaze to the ground, so I glance up at the stipes. The upright post is rough-hewn and nothing like the skilled craftmanship of my Joseph and Jesus. The horizontal cross board lies on the parched ground, and a flickering hope flashes through me like icy wind on a hot day: They have taken down my son's cross. Pilate's scourging, the beatings, the humiliations have satisfied the crowd's fiendish appetite.

Roman soldiers pass behind us, stealing from me the spark of relief at Jesus' absence. They are of the Roman 10th Legion, mercenaries known for brutality. I try not to think of the men we have often seen hanging on crosses as we walk the road below. Crucifixion is the worst form of execution, so horrendous that it is against the law for Romans to crucify a Roman.

A young Roman soldier trips in his rush to the cross and drops one of the long, square-sided nails he carries. Other uniformed men shove him aside as the crowd shifts and heads turn. "There! Over there!" Cries break out: "Crucify! Crucify!"

Then I see my beautiful Jesus, his face so battered, blood covering his forehead, nose, and cheeks I have kissed since his miraculous birth. And yet . . . light still shines from those eyes. He is the Light of the World, even as they throw him onto the cross, stretching his arms out on the cross plank, soldiers pinning his wrists as if he were fighting. More soldiers move in with spikes and hammers not unlike those I have seen in the hands of my husband and my son.

Is it our Father's grace that I can no longer see? Too many tears blind my eyes . . . blind as the many blind eyes healed by the touch of Jesus. I can hear, though—the clang, CLANG! Endless pounding into hands that healed, feet that walked over rocks and briars to carry the message of peace and salvation to all.

PONDERING . . .

1.) Have you ever watched someone you love suffer? In what ways can we "watch" the Crucifixion this Easter in order to appreciate the cost of our salvation?

2.) This Easter, how can you "stay at the cross" like the faithful women who followed Jesus to his Crucifixion? Religious holidays can open natural opportunities to talk about God. Ponder what you might say to a relative or friend this Easter to help them understand what the cross of Jesus means to you.

3.) Can you think of a time you wish you had talked to someone about Christ? What do you think kept you from speaking? Do you remember a time when you risked speaking out for Christ? What happened?

4.) Anguish is severe struggling with pain and suffering in the past; agony is struggle in the present. The only time *anguish* appears in the New Testament is when Jesus prays in Gethsemane before his arrest, when his sweat became like great drops of blood. Ponder why Jesus felt anguish while praying.

Dear God,

Thank you for sending your Son to suffer the agony of the Crucifixion to take away my sins. Give me strength to stand up for you and share what you've done for me.

Day 27

MARY MAGDALENE

Seeking

Near the cross of Jesus stood his mother, his mother's sister, Mary the wife of Clopas, and Mary Magdalene.

(John 19:25, NIV)

"He saved others," they scoffed, "but he can't save himself! So he is the King of Israel, is he? Let him come down from the cross right now, and we will believe in him!"

(Matthew 27:42, NLT)

Thus says the Lord: Stand at the crossroads and look, and ask for the ancient paths, where the good way lies; and walk in it, and find rest for your souls.

(Jeremiah 6:16)

"Come," my heart says, "seek his face!"
Your face, LORD, do I seek.

(Psalm 27:8)

Look to him, and be radiant,
so your faces shall never be ashamed.

(Psalm 34:5)

MARY MAGDALENE
Seeking

I cannot bear to imagine my life without Jesus beside me, leading as my Good Shepherd. Please, Adonai-Rohi, The Lord is my Shepherd! Even from here, where I huddle in the back of the crowd with other women whose lives are new because of Christ, I smell burning flesh and hair of sacrificial animals. "Susanna, I must go nearer."

She nods, and I elbow through a sea of vile traitors calling for the death of the One who gave me life. Susanna rests a hand to my back as she tries to keep up. "Magdalene," she shouts, "Joanna says Judas was the one who betrayed Jesus."

I do not slow my pace, but keep struggling to pass a group of Sadducees, all enjoying themselves and taunting Jesus. Soon, I have lost track of Susanna.

A well-fed Pharisee, his gray beard curled past his neck, the tassels of his garment so long he is in danger of tripping, shouts, "You, who claimed you would destroy our temple in three days, save yourself!" On his forehead, he wears a broad phylactery, the box no doubt filled with scriptures that hold no meaning for his hard heart.

Finally, I reach the front, where Mary, mother of Jesus, stands with John. Their tunics are not unlike—John's lighter of weight and darker in color than Mary's long, faded goat's hair. One arm crosses her chest as if she fears her organs might fall out. I long to help her, though I can see no path to do so. "Mary?"

She turns to me with eyes of compassion, then back to her son. I look in time to see Jesus, nailed to the cross, hoisted to the sky, only to be dropped with the cross into a hole with a thud that draws groans, even from a crowd of hate. Crucified men on either side of Jesus begin hurling abuse at him. My head buzzes, and waves of heat make me feel faint.

"When the Israelites complained to Moses in the desert, El Shaddai sent poisonous snakes that killed many." Mary might have been storytelling with children. "Then the Lord told Moses to make a bronze serpent and set it on a pole. Anyone bitten could simply look at the serpent and live."

John leans down and says something but is drowned out by a man bulky as a feed bag. "Crucify! Crucify him!" His spit flies out through rotted teeth.

Mary stares into the angry faces cursing her son. "Oh, Magdalene, all they have to do is look to their Savior."

PONDERING . . .

1.) Imagine you're Magdalene or one of the other women who stayed at the cross with Jesus. What would you have said to those shouting for Jesus' Crucifixion? During this Easter celebration, what can you say that might help another believer, or someone struggling to believe?

2.) Do you believe that Jesus' purpose in coming to earth was to set a good example or to die? How does looking to Jesus and accepting him seem too easy a salvation?

3.) Why did God the Father allow his Son to be mistreated to such a degree? If Jesus had died without suffering, would he have paid for sin?

4.) Jesus invites us to look to him and seek his face. How can you look to Jesus and seek his face as you celebrate Easter?

Dear God,
Help me to always look to you
and seek your face.

JESUS' SEVEN WORDS FROM THE CROSS

The last words of anyone are important, "famous last words." The last words of Jesus Christ, the Son of God, are worthy of more attention than can possibly be given in this book.

The next seven devotionals focus on Jesus' seven last utterances. I've given each to one of the women who journeyed with Jesus or had her life changed by him. Since we're not told in Scripture which woman heard which words, I've chosen one woman who would have needed to hear these specific words from Jesus.

Then Jesus said, "Father, forgive them, for they do not know what they are doing."
And they cast lots to divide his clothing.

(Luke 23:34)

He replied, "Truly I tell you, today you will be with me in paradise."

(Luke 23:43)

When Jesus saw his mother and the disciple whom he loved standing beside her, he said to his mother, "Woman, here is your son." Then he said to the disciple, "Here is your mother." And from that hour the disciple took her into his own home.

(John 19:26–27)

At three o'clock Jesus cried out with a loud voice, "Eloi, Eloi, lema sabachthani?" which means, "My God, my God, why have you forsaken me?"

(Mark 15:34)

After this, when Jesus knew that all was now finished, he said (in order to fulfill the scripture), "I am thirsty."

(John 19:28)

When he had received the drink, Jesus said, "It is finished."

(John 19:30, NIV)

Then Jesus, crying out with a loud voice, said,
"Father, into your hands I commend my spirit."
Having said this, he breathed his last.

(Luke 23:46)

SALOME

Forgive

Then Jesus said, "Father, forgive them, for they do not know what they are doing." And they cast lots to divide his clothing.
(Luke 23:34)

All the prophets testify about him that everyone who believes in him receives forgiveness of sins through his name.
(Acts 10:43)

I am writing to you, little children, because your sins are forgiven on account of his name.
(1 John 2:12)

Make allowance for each other's faults, and forgive anyone who offends you.
Remember, the Lord forgave you,
so you must forgive others.
(Colossians 3:13, NLT)

SALOME
Forgive

It has taken time for me to believe that Jesus forgives me for my haughty request. Kind Zebedee has teased me about my inability to admit when I am wrong. But how wrong I was to demand my sons rule in Jesus' kingdom! I see my sin and have truly repented. Yet I understand it is by grace that Jesus forgives me, not because I have finally come to my senses.

"Liar!" shouts a man whose graying beard sprawls like a sea creature on his face. "I have read the Law and the Prophets. The Messiah will live forever! You will not last the night."

I reach Mary and see that John stands with her. I see no other disciple, only Mary, wife of Clopas, Mary, mother of James and Joses, Magdalene, and many women in the crowd. I have avoided Mary as I have everyone who witnessed my pride and shame when making my foolish request. Mary's agony has aged her lovely face, stretching her cheeks while creasing her forehead. And yet, a peace covers her, a glow of warmth and inner calm.

"Mary, I am so sorry." How inadequate is this true statement of my heart. I am sorry for my selfish ambition, for what unfolds before us. "Were I a man, I would rescue Jesus!" Even to myself I sound like the old Salome—filled with pride, emptied of humility.

Mary turns to me with compassion, and her misery becomes mine. Only then do I look up the small hill and see Jesus, held to the cross by spikes, expertly driven to sever nerves and bring more pain. How quick I was to boast that James and John could drink of this cup!

I do not know if minutes or hours have passed when I hear Jesus' voice. "Father, forgive them, for they know not what they do."

His words crash into my soul. "Mary, how can he forgive his torturers? They don't deserve it."

Looking only at her son, Mary answers, "None of us deserve forgiveness, Salome."

"My father always said, 'I will forgive you, but I'll never forget.' His words live in my mind. How could my prideful request not live in the mind of your Son?"

Mary shakes her head. "Adonai told Jeremiah: 'For I will forgive their iniquity, and I will remember their sin no more.'"

"He forgives and forgets?" I let the words wash over the words of my father.

She nods, then looks back to Jesus. I am as undeserving of such complete forgiveness as the soldier holding the bloodied hammer. *Thank you, Jehovah Shalom, Lord of Peace, for giving me the peace of true forgiveness.*

PONDERING . . .

1.) Luke records Jesus' first words on the cross: *"Father, forgive them, for they know not what they do."* Why do you think Jesus utters this prayer before saying anything else? How regularly do you ask or thank God for his forgiveness?

2.) Watching the Crucifixion, Salome must have realized what she had asked for her sons. Have you ever asked God for things you're grateful he did not give you? How has that experience transformed the way you pray?

3.) Salome probably carried guilt for her prideful request. Do you feel guilty even when you know you're forgiven? What can you do this week to let God help you with guilt?

4.) Jesus asked for forgiveness—not for himself since he was without sin—but for his executioners. Is there anyone you need to forgive? How can you "forget" when someone has hurt you? Should you forgive someone who doesn't even want your forgiveness?

Dear God,
Thank you, thank you for always forgiving me.
Help me forgive and forget, the way you
forgive and forget my sins.

Day 29

SUSANNA

Paradise-Bound

One of the criminals who were hanged there *was hurling abuse at Him, saying, "Are You not the Christ? Save Yourself and us!" But the other responded, and rebuking him, said, "Do you not even fear God, since you are under the same sentence of condemnation? And we indeed are* suffering *justly, for we are receiving what we deserve for our crimes; but this man has done nothing wrong." And he was saying, "Jesus, remember me when You come into Your kingdom!" And He said to him, "Truly I say to you, today you will be with Me in Paradise."*

(Luke 23:39–43, NASB)

To everyone who conquers, I will give permission to eat from the tree of life that is in the paradise of God.

(Revelation 2:7b)

But our citizenship is in heaven, and it is from there that we are expecting a Savior, the Lord Jesus Christ.

(Philippians 3:20)

SUSANNA

Paradise-Bound

Though Jesus and his mother made me feel part of the family, I now find myself standing apart from Mary, Salome, Magdalene, and many others, like Joanna, in the crowd. If I have ever belonged to any group, it is with these who love Jesus as I do. Yet I fear I will never have the deep sense of belonging I know the others carry with them.

I know I belong to Jesus. But when he is gone. . . .

I risk a glance to the hill and take in the red-black stripes covering Jesus' body, his swollen eyes, the trembling of his legs as he tries to push himself up to keep his lungs from being crushed. He wheezes, then gasps for air.

Overriding the ragged breath of the Messiah are the voices of the thieves on either side, shouting obscenities, mocking the roaring Lion of the tribe of Judah. It is an insult for the Lord to be near these criminals, between them, suffering as if one of them.

The one whose skin is so sunbaked he must have stolen in day as well as night, shouts, "If you're the Messiah, save yourself and us!"

After a time, while the thief continues to spew foul words like daggers at Jesus, the other yells, "Stop! Don't you even fear God? We're getting what we deserve, but this man has done nothing wrong."

I am surprised to see Jesus smile. Missing and broken teeth, split lips, and bloody nose cannot dampen the power of that smile. The joy in his eyes has the effect of leading me by still waters and restoring my soul.

The rapt thief coughs, and blood drips from his mouth. "Jesus, remember me when you come into your kingdom!"

Jesus utters something which the dryness of his throat renders unintelligible. He licks his lips and tries again. "Truly I say to you, today you will be with Me in Paradise."

I gasp. With Jesus' words, I am once again touched by my Savior's gracious love. This thief has done nothing to earn salvation, but he is promised Paradise today! He contributes nothing but faith in the Son of God. I, too, have done nothing to earn salvation. I may not have committed the thief's crimes, but how often I have complained on our journeys as if only I ached from sleeping on hard ground. In my heart I complained of swollen feet, Joanna's cooking, Salome's untimely absences. But because Jesus is on that cross, both the believing thief and I truly belong with Jesus in *Paradise*.

PONDERING . . .

1.) We have little background on the two thieves crucified with Jesus. Imagine that you're the taunting criminal. Why are you blaming and cursing Jesus? Then ponder whether you sometimes blame God when things go wrong.

2.) Even in Jesus' final hours on earth, he cared deeply about leading someone—a criminal—to salvation. If you knew today would be your last day on earth, is there someone you'd talk to about salvation?

3.) The repentant thief reasoned that unlike the righteous Jesus, the two thieves were getting what they deserved. Ponder whether or not you'd like to get what you deserve.

4.) If you were the only person in the world, do you believe Jesus would have died for you? Why do you think he would, or wouldn't?

Dear God,
Thank you that because of your Son, I belong.
Help me to see each person as someone you
want with us in Paradise.

Day 30

MARY, MOTHER OF JESUS

Provision

Now beside the cross of Jesus stood His mother, His mother's sister, Mary the wife of Clopas, and Mary Magdalene. So when Jesus saw His mother, and the disciple whom He loved standing nearby, He said to His mother, "Woman, behold, your son!" Then He said to the disciple, "Behold, your mother!" And from that hour the disciple took her into his own household.

(John 19:25–27, NASB)

And whoever does not provide for relatives, and especially for family members, has denied the faith and is worse than an unbeliever.

(1 Timothy 5:8)

And my God will fully satisfy every need of yours according to his riches in glory in Christ Jesus.

(Philippians 4:19)

MARY, MOTHER OF JESUS

Provision

"If you are so powerful, come down from that cross!" shouts a priestly young man who pushes in front of me. He wears a linen garment over the top of the tunic to keep himself pure. His blue ephod is richly embroidered, and his white turban winds around his head and trails onto his back. He carries a jewel-encrusted pouch that must hold wealth.

And then there is my son, whose life has left him with the clothes on his back, clothing now being divided among his executioners: sandals, head covering, garments, and a belt not deemed worthy of fighting over. But the soldiers decide to cast lots for the seamless tunic I wove for Jesus. What good would it be divided by four?

The young priest is not finished. "Come down from the cross, and I will believe in you!"

El Roi, the God who sees, how am I to survive among these false leaders without Jesus' watchful care over me? A calm I do not feel takes control of me. "Do you not yet understand?" I ask, amazed at such ignorance from a leader of Israel.

His eyes are black slits, and his face takes on the appearance of a serpent insulted by an ant. "Did you speak to me?"

Magdalene steps between us. "She did. And you should be grateful since she speaks the truth. Jesus could call ten thousand angels to take him from that cross."

The man tries to laugh, but seems unused to the process. "Then why would he not leap from the cross and save himself?"

John, standing beside me, begins to intervene, but I must speak. "Because of you." My voice contains no accusation. And without warning, I want this man to understand and believe.

"You blame me?" he demands.

I shake my head. "If you offered to release my son, he would not leave the cross."

"Jesus is staying on that cross for you. This is his life's purpose," Magdalene explains.

I read the priest's consternation and feel the compassion of Christ. "Do you not yet understand the Scriptures or the power of God? The Messiah comes to die for the sins of us all?"

The man's face contorts, and I believe his soul is tormented between fear and ignorance as he settles on silence and disappears into the crowd.

"Mary!" Salome points to the cross, where Jesus is staring down at John.

The world ceases to exist as I look to my son and hear him speak. "Woman, behold, your son!" And to John, he says, "Behold your mother!"

I hear a tiny gasp from Salome, John's actual mother, but she immediately leans across John and hugs me. John weeps. How he loves my son! My own tears flow, not merely from relief that Jesus has once again provided for my needs, but that even in the middle of his darkest hour, Jesus, Jehovah Jireh, *The Lord will Provide*, is thinking of me.

PONDERING . . .

1.) How do you think Mary needed to provide for Jesus as a young man? Later, in what ways do you think Jesus provided for Mary? How have others provided for you? In what ways do you provide for those around you?

2.) Jehovah-Jireh means "God will provide." It's the name of God that Abraham used when he climbed the mountain to sacrifice his own son. When Isaac asked where the sacrificial lamb was, Abraham told him, "God will provide," and God did (Genesis 22:14). How has God provided for you in the past? What are you trusting God to provide right now?

3.) Psalm 68:6, NLT, promises: "God places the lonely in families." As Jesus' followers traveled with him, relationships deepened, and they provided for one another. Is there someone God may be asking you to invite into your family circle or to care for as if they were relatives?

4.) Have you ever felt as if God were not providing? Do you have any fears about how God will get you through the next phase of your life on earth? How could Easter give you confidence and security?

Dear God,
Thank you for the many ways you provide for me every day! Help me to be more generous and provide for the poor and homeless.

Day 31

MARY OF BETHANY

Forsaken

When it was noon, darkness came over the whole land until three in the afternoon. At three o'clock Jesus cried out with a loud voice, "Eloi, Eloi, lema sabachthani?" which means, "My God, my God, why have you forsaken me?"

(Mark 15:33–34)

All we like sheep have gone astray; we have all turned to our own way, and the LORD has laid on him the iniquity of us all.

(Isaiah 53:6)

My God, my God, why have you forsaken me? Why are you so far from helping me,
from the words of my groaning?

(Psalm 22:1)

MARY OF BETHANY
Forsaken

Since nine this morning, I have watched the horror of crucifying the Son of God. I am thankful that I convinced Martha and Lazarus to remain home. As I left, my sister said, "Bring Jesus when you return." When I gave her a knowing look, she added, "He is the Resurrection and the Life, Mary. I will ready the meal for our friends."

How I long to sit at Jesus' feet and listen for any word from my Teacher! His mother, Mary, does not look away from the cross. The most tender woman I know is also the strongest.

Suddenly, something changes in the air. For three hours the sun has beaten down with a fiery heat. Now the sun darkens, as if covering its face in shame.

For the next three hours, in this unnatural darkness, I listen to my Lord struggle for breath, with rasping as of meal grinding under a stone wheel. He must put his weight onto his bloodied feet, nailed to the cross. This painful move allows his lungs to take in air over bruised ribs. But unable to sustain the weight, he collapses and empties of air—renewing the wicked cycle of death.

What must it feel like to experience, for the first time, the weight of sin—taking on all of our worst deeds and thoughts, those of the Babylonians and Assyrians, the Romans and

Jews? Does he also bear all future sins of a world that rejects him? No physical pain compares to what must now be taking place in the depth of his soul.

"Did he speak?" a Roman voice not far from me asks.

Then out of darkness, I hear the Son of God cry out in a miraculously loud voice: "Eloi, Eloi, lema sabachthani?" It is the language of his childhood, Aramaic. "My God, my God, why have you forsaken me?" He addresses God as would any Jew, not with the intimate "Abba."

The words tear at my heart. *Forsaken.* Abandoned. Since before Creation, Jesus has been One with his Father. Now, because of our sin, Jesus is separated from God the Father.

Two young women lament behind me. "I followed him from Galilee and saw him do miracles. Why would Elohim now forsake him?"

I turn to them. "Jesus is bearing the sins of the whole world so we can spend eternity with Elohim. It is our sin that now severs Jesus from his Father. He is paying the price to redeem us."

"That isn't fair!" the wide-eyed woman retorts.

I shake my head. "No. Fair would be for Jesus to return to heaven and leave us to die in our unforgiven sin, with no hope of salvation. Is that the Jesus you followed?"

They withdraw from me and join others down the path away from Golgotha, leaving me alone. I am watching the supreme sacrifice that fulfills prophecies. This moment is why my Savior came, the moment for which I anointed him.

Pondering . . .

1.) What more modern words would you have for “forsaken?” When have you felt this way?

2.) This Easter, do you know, or suspect, anyone who might feel forsaken—someone who has experienced loss? What can you do to help?

3.) Many Christians use an acronym for GRACE: God’s Riches At Christ’s Expense. Ponder in your own words what that means to you.

4.) How could Easter help you focus on Jesus’ true purpose on earth. Was “Good Friday,” when Jesus was crucified, truly good? Why or why not?

Dear God,
Thank you for giving new life to me.
Use me to help others experience your grace.

Day 32

SAMARITAN WOMAN

Thirst

After this, when Jesus knew that all was now finished, he said (in order to fulfill the scripture), "I am thirsty." A jar full of sour wine was standing there. So they put a sponge full of the wine on a branch of hyssop and held it to his mouth.

(John 19:28–29)

They gave me poison for food, and for my thirst they gave me vinegar to drink.

(Psalm 69:21)

On the last day of the festival, the great day, while Jesus was standing there, he cried out, "Let anyone who is thirsty come to me, and let the one who believes in me drink. As the scripture has said, 'Out of the believer's heart shall flow rivers of living water.'"

(John 7:37–38)

SAMARITAN WOMAN

Thirst

I did not believe that the land of Judea, the City of David, could turn on the Messiah. It is we Samaritans who are outcasts. In hopes of seeing Jesus, a number of us set out to celebrate Passover in Jerusalem, rather than Mount Gerizim.

But now, here I stand before a tortured man unable to lift his head from a cross. Since the day Jesus came to Jacob's well and offered me living water, I have overflowed with joy given me by the Son of God. In Sychar I have told everyone who would listen—and many who would not—about the kind Messiah, filled with grace and truth.

Now in the dark and surrounded by Roman soldiers who steal unholy glances at me, I cannot stop the tears. They burn in my chest, overflowing as once joy did.

Beside me, a young soldier stabs a sponge onto a hyssop branch and dips it into the bucket of sour wine, which is never far from soldiers. He holds it up as if to give Jesus a drink.

I jump aside as a mounted officer rides up. "No! Stop! The man is calling for ELI-jah, one of their prophets. Let's see whether Elijah will come to save him."

How foolish they are, these men who gladly crucify the Messiah of God! *Eli, Eli* echoes the prophetic Psalm: *My God, My God!*

How often I have replayed my first meeting with Jesus, who asked me for a drink—me, a woman and a Samaritan. Was it his asking that gave me a rare moment of feeling needed? So amazed was I when he revealed himself as the Messiah that I left the well without giving him a drink. Oh that I had that water at this moment! I would dare any man here, Roman or Jew, to keep me from climbing that cross and offering my drink.

There is movement from the cross. Jesus, in what must be an extraordinary gathering of strength, lifts his head. My eyes block the surrounding darkness and perceive the light of the Savior reaching out to me. My mind shuts out every voice but his.

"I am thirsty."

His words reverberate in my heart as I picture him—not on the cross, but grinning at the well, explaining to me the meaning of living water. I had thirsted for years, foolishly quenching my desires with empty attempts at love. I had no idea what love was until I met Jesus.

Thirst. Could it be that Jesus has said this for my sake?

I have drunk the eternal, living water offered me. There are many questions I cannot answer, so much I do not understand. Yet I believe. And I thirst for no one but my Lord.

Pondering . . .

1.) After three hours under a beating sun, dehydrated from loss of blood, likely having taken his last drink at the Last Supper, Jesus must have ached with thirst. Was there ever a time when you were so thirsty it hurt? When you finally drank, what did that feel like?

2.) What have you thirsted for in the past? Love, popularity, success, security, revenge, or . . . ? Are you thirsting for something now? Ponder how getting what you want might affect your relationship with God.

3.) The Samaritan woman changed and started thirsting for God. If you're thirsting for something that God may not have chosen for you, how can you switch to "living water"?

4.) What do light and darkness usually mean as metaphors? Ponder in what ways Christ is your Light. How can you help someone move from darkness into the light this Easter season?

Dear God,
Thank you for the promise of eternal life in you.
Help me thirst only for you.

Day 33

MARY OF BETHANY

Finished

When Jesus had received the wine, he said,
"It is finished."

(John 19:30)

Unlike the other high priests, he has no need to offer sacrifices day after day, first for his own sins and then for those of the people; this he did once for all when he offered himself.

(Hebrews 7:27)

Then he said to me, "It is done! I am the Alpha and the Omega, the Beginning and the End. To the thirsty I will give water as a gift from the spring of the water of life."

(Revelation 21:6)

I have fought the good fight; I have finished the race; I have kept the faith.

(2 Timothy 4:7)

MARY OF BETHANY
Finished

I am at the edge of the fast-dissipating crowd when Jesus calls on his last earthly strength to proclaim, "It is finished." His voice rises above the thunder.

Finished? Finished teaching me, a woman disciple who wants nothing more than to sit at his feet? Finished with the laughter that brought with it joy and peace?

I have known the Messiah must die. I anointed him for burial. He has told us many times that his death would pay for our sins, setting us free. And yet, I do not feel free. I am more sorrowful than at the death of my brother, when Jesus shared my tears.

Near the cross I see Mary and Magdalene, Mary, wife of Clopas, Salome, and others, but I will remain no longer. It is finished, and I must bring this news to Martha and Lazarus.

• • •

Martha is waiting when I arrive disheveled and wet; the earth has shaken, and heaven poured out power with sounds of rocks cracking and earth splitting. My sister covers me with her shawl and pulls me inside, glancing behind as if expecting Jesus and all the disciples. I smell lamb and her special bean meal, fresh bread. But I see by her face that she understands.

I cannot hold back tears so loud that Lazarus rushes in from the courtyard. "Oh, Lazarus, Jesus said it is finished. He may have said more as he breathed his last, but I had to come home."

My brother draws his sisters into his strong arms.

Martha has no tears. "It is finished, Mary, because Jesus finished it. He will rise again."

I look up at Martha, sharing the warmth of her wisdom. Jesus will rise again. The assurance of this promise changes everything and fills me with hope. I see it now. I picture Pilate's sign tacked to the cross, saying only "King of the Jews." For all others, the sign must list their crimes and offenses. I have seen Matthew write *tetelestai*, "Paid in Full," "It is finished," on completed documents. These words of Jesus are victorious. The Son of God paid in full and finished his work on earth.

Only this no longer feels like the end—more like the beginning. "He is finished," I whisper, "for now."

PONDERING . . .

1.) The apostle Paul wrote to Timothy that he, Paul, had "finished the race." What do you think he meant? Do you believe that you have a "race" God wants you to finish? What things help you keep on the racetrack? What things don't?

2.) Christ died for all our sins. Do you rank sins—some really bad and others no big deal? Is worry a big-deal sin or just something we all do? What does worrying say about your relationship with God?

3.) Can you go a day without sinning? Try to keep track of your sins for one day (worry, thoughts, words, little lies, laziness, pride, a lack of gratitude). How many times did you ask God for forgiveness?

4.) Explain to someone what Jesus meant by "It is finished." What's been God's plan since before Creation? Ponder what it has taken for God to rescue us.

Dear God,
Thank you for finishing your
work for my salvation.
Show me the path to finishing
the work you want me to do.

Day 34

MARY, MOTHER OF JESUS

Spirit

It was now about noon, and darkness came over the whole land until three in the afternoon, while the sun's light failed, and the curtain of the temple was torn in two. Then Jesus, crying out with a loud voice, said, "Father, into your hands I commend my spirit." Having said this, he breathed his last.

(Luke 23:44–46)

When the centurion saw what had taken place, he praised God and said, "Certainly this man was innocent." And when all the crowds who had gathered there for this spectacle saw what had taken place, they returned home, beating their breasts.

(Luke 23:47–49)

Now when the centurion and those with him, who were keeping watch over Jesus, saw the earthquake and what took place, they were terrified and said, "Truly this man was God's Son!"

(Matthew 27:54)

MARY, MOTHER OF JESUS

Spirit

My son hangs on the cross, no longer able to push himself up to gain breath.

My own breath fails, drowned in his agony. All day I have wished I could take my son's place on the torturous cross, though I know how feeble would be the exchange. I have my own sins to die for and cannot offer my life to pay for the sins of others.

When Gabriel visited me in Nazareth with the news that I would bear the Messiah, I said, "Let it be with me according to your word." Would I have said those words had I realized where they would lead?

Each year Joseph told the story of Passover, when faithful Jews, slaves in Egypt, dipped hyssop branches into the blood of lambs and sprinkled blood on their doorposts so the angel of death would pass over the house and spare their firstborn sons. Adonai, can you yet spare mine? Yours?

"Look at that!" cries a centurion beneath the cross.

Jesus miraculously summons strength to cry out, "Father, into your hands I commit my spirit!"

"Oh, my precious Jesus!" I look from woman to woman, followers of my son, who have traveled with him from Galilee and beyond. "Did you hear, my sisters? Jesus gave up his spirit. No one took it from him. He has committed his spirit into his Father's hands!"

Beside the cross, a Roman centurion bursts into praise and shouts, "Truly this man was God's Son!"

I feel the earth shake and hear the cries of the mob. Crowds beat their breasts and scurry away like locusts caught in a current within the Jordan River. Rocks split and tumble from Golgotha. The ground opens, threatening to swallow us as in the time of Korah's rebellion when the leaders fell through cracks in the earth.

John puts an arm around my shoulder. "Mary, we must go home."

And I, with no fear, go with him, knowing my son has provided all I will ever need.

Pondering . . .

1.) Do you believe that a sin you'll commit tomorrow has already been forgiven? Why, or why not? Does this knowledge keep you from giving in to that sin or encourage you to go ahead with it?

2.) What do the words "Once saved, always saved" mean to you? What about "the assurance of salvation"? What's the relationship between salvation, sin, and good works?

3.) Do you ever feel like there's a big sin in your past that couldn't possibly be forgiven? Ponder your answer and your feelings about past sins. Is there a difference between the fact of forgiveness and the feeling of forgiveness?

4.) Currently, deeply different political views have divided Christian communities, churches, and even families. Disagreements and judgmental attitudes can turn hostile. Jesus taught that the world would know we're Christians by our love. How can Christians remain "one in the Spirit" and show brotherly love, even in political or cultural turmoil?

Dear God,
Help me to thank you more often for paying for my sin. Help me show abiding, forgiving love to others.

Day 35

JOANNA, WIFE OF CHUZA

Torn

Then Jesus cried again with a loud voice and breathed his last. At that moment the curtain of the temple was torn in two, from top to bottom. The earth shook, and the rocks were split.

(Matthew 27:50–51)

There were two rooms in that Tabernacle. In the first room were a lampstand, a table, and sacred loaves of bread on the table. This room was called the Holy Place. Then there was a curtain, and behind the curtain was the second room called the Most Holy Place.

(Hebrews 9:2–3, NLT)

He [Jesus] entered once for all into the holy place, not with the blood of goats and calves but with his own blood, thus obtaining eternal redemption.

(Hebrews 9:12)

And so, dear brothers and sisters, we can boldly
enter heaven's Most Holy Place
because of the blood of Jesus.

(Hebrews 10:19, NLT)

He keeps all their bones; not one of them
will be broken.

(Psalm 34:20)

They will look on me whom they have pierced and mourn for him as for an only son. They will grieve bitterly for him as for a firstborn son who has died.

(Zechariah 12:10b, NLT)

JOANNA, WIFE OF CHUZA

Torn

I have come to the Temple to beg others, including Adonai, to free Jesus, to take him down from the cross and let him go. Barely have I reached the Court of the Gentiles when the ground beneath me shakes. I fear my old weakness has returned until I hear the cries of others.

Religious leaders race from the Court of the Priests, leaving sacrificial fires aflame. They shove through the Beautiful Gate of the soreg stone wall dividing Israelites from the rest of humanity. I shout questions at them which they do not answer.

A servant from Herod's palace takes a moment to answer me. "The curtain! The one separating the Holy Place from the Most Holy Place—it has ripped in two, top to bottom!" He escapes before I can ask more. Only the high priest once a year may enter the Most Holy Place behind the curtain, where he confesses his own sins and that of the people. The curtain is at least four inches thick and sixty feet high. No one could tear that curtain . . . top to bottom . . . except—

I fight crowds all the way to Golgotha, pushing through mobs fleeing as if from a flaming amphitheater, crying out in Hebrew, Aramaic, Greek, and languages unknown to me.

While still far away, I see Jesus hanging lifeless between two others. Is this what I knew I would find? My heart will not accept it, and even my mind rebels, sending me instead visions of the strong Messiah overturning tables, chasing money-changers from the Temple. I call up a vision of my loving Jesus grinning as he healed me before I even realized it, right before he stormed the Temple.

"Joanna, where were you?" Magdalene runs to me, followed by Salome, Mary, wife of Clopas, the other Mary, and many women who traveled with us from Galilee.

I am quick to answer. "I bring news from the Temple, where all is chaos. The curtain separating the Most Holy Place has torn in two, top to bottom."

Salome's eyes darken, perhaps with suspicion. "The curtain that reaches ceiling to floor? Torn top to bottom? But how?"

Mary, mother of James and Joses, whispers, "It is Elohim, the All-Powerful One. Perhaps he is angry at the death of his Son?"

"He is not angry," Magdalene says, her eyes shining. "God sent his Son to die for our sin, and Jesus did what he came to do. Even the curtain keeping us from Adonai's presence has been torn away. Now, we can enter the Holiest Place and go directly to our God."

After a long silence I am told of more prophecies fulfilled. Though the legs of the two thieves were broken by soldiers to hasten their deaths, no one had to break the bones of Jesus.

Salome reports that a soldier thrust his sword, piercing Jesus' side. "Mary told us of the old man, Simeon, who prophesied that a sword would pierce her heart also."

I study the faces of these women I have come to love. "We will pray for Mary's pain with the confidence that Jehovah-Rapha, The Lord Who Heals, hears us. The barrier between us has been removed."

PONDERING . . .

1.) Do you believe you can talk with God one-on-one? What steps could you take at Easter to lead you into a deeper relationship with Jesus?

2.) Why do you think Jesus' male disciples, except John, failed to show up at the Crucifixion? Imagine their thoughts and rationale. Have you ever stayed away from conflict for the same reasons you imagine the apostles did?

3.) Picture a pipe that leads from you to God. Imagine that pipe is clogged. You're still a Christian, but you can't seem to get through to God. Is anything blocking your "pipe" now? How can you unclog it?

4.) Why do you think Jesus seemed angry when he cleansed the Temple, overturning the tables of unscrupulous money-changers, but forgave his torturers, showing no anger on the cross? In your own life, can you distinguish "righteous anger" from plain old anger?

Dear God,
Show me every sin that keeps me from being close to you. Thank you for loving me so much that you forgive me.

Day 36

MARY MAGDALENE

Loyalty

Do not let loyalty and faithfulness forsake you; bind them around your neck;
write them on the tablet of your heart.

(Proverbs 3:3)

After these things, Joseph of Arimathea, who was a disciple of Jesus, though a secret one because of his fear of the Jews, asked Pilate to let him take away the body of Jesus. Pilate gave him permission, so he came and removed his body. Nicodemus, who had at first come to Jesus by night, also came, bringing a mixture of myrrh and aloes, weighing about a hundred pounds. They took the body of Jesus and wrapped it with the spices in linen cloths, according to the burial custom of the Jews. Now there was a garden in the place where he was crucified, and in the garden there was a new tomb in which no one had ever been laid. And so, because it was the Jewish day of Preparation and the tomb was nearby, they laid Jesus there.

(John 19:38–42)

He had done no wrong and had never deceived anyone. But he was buried like a criminal; he was put in a rich man's grave.

(Isaiah 53:9, NLT)

MARY MAGDALENE
Loyalty

I will not allow Jesus to hang on that cross over the Sabbath." I mean this though I see no disciple to help, not even Peter, only the women, who have no voice with authorities.

I have forgotten about Susanna until she speaks. She hands each of us a fig, reminding me how long I have gone without eating. She points to Nicodemus, the Pharisee who visited Jesus by night for fear of the other religious leaders. "Jesus believed Nicodemus to be sincere in his seeking. Perhaps he will help? Remember how he struggled when Jesus told him, 'You must be born again'?"

Joanna nods toward a Pharisee exchanging words with Nicodemus. "Joseph of Arimathea is a wealthy member of the Council, who did not consent to their decision." She moves in closer, then rejoins us. "Joseph asked Pilate for Jesus' body and was granted permission to bury Jesus—not in a criminal's grave—but in the new grave of the Arimathean."

"Pilate could have executed him as a follower, just for asking," Salome says.

I fight nausea as we watch the men work to free Jesus from the cross. "I want to help them."

Only Joanna's hand on my arm stays me. "Magdalene, it is well. See how they wrap his body with the linen shroud and skillfully place the cloth over the face? Nicodemus' mixture of myrrh and aloes is of great weight."

Salome shakes her head. "They will not have the time before sundown to properly cleanse and anoint him. Aloes are fine, as is myrrh. But what about proper spices for the odor?"

How can we be speaking of these things? I want to yet run to Jesus, to be buried with him. But that is not where my Good Shepherd calls me. "We will bring spices and ointments when the Sabbath ends. But first, we must follow them and see where they lay our Lord."

• • •

Mary, mother of James, Salome, and I sleep in the home of one of the women of Jerusalem. We have readied oils and spices bought with coinage from Joanna and Susanna. Sleep, however, does not come for me. My mind spins with questions: How will we enter the tomb, now sealed and blocked by a large round stone? It must be pushed from a groove cut into the opening of the cave, then rolled up the incline, a feat requiring several men. Then there is the problem of the soldiers. Joanna explained that Pilate agreed to post special guards at the tomb under penalty of death, should one fall asleep.

Hours pass, and I find no answers, only more questions. How am I to live without Jesus?

My only conclusion: I cannot wait for the light of dawn.

PONDERING . . .

1.) Many of us have regrets after a person's death—what we should have said, what we might have done differently. How can you deal with those feelings? How can you help others with their regrets?

2.) Do you believe, know as fact, that you will go to heaven when you die? How can you know for sure?

3.) Why did Jesus have to die? Would it have been enough for him to come and set a good example of how we should live? Couldn't he have returned to heaven without enduring the torture of the cross?

4.) On the journey through villages, Jesus told his followers: "If any wish to come after me, let them deny themselves and take up their cross daily and follow me" (Luke 9:23). Ponder what it means for you to take up your cross. What is your personal cross?

Dear God,
Please help me always to be loyal to you.
Thank you for your never-ending
faithfulness to me.

Day 37

MARY MAGDALENE

Resurrection!

Early on the first day of the week, while it was still dark, Mary Magdalene came to the tomb and saw that the stone had been removed from the tomb. So she ran and went to Simon Peter and the other disciple, the one whom Jesus loved, and said to them, "They have taken the Lord out of the tomb, and we do not know where they have laid him."

(John 20:1–2)

And very early on the first day of the week, when the sun had risen, they went to the tomb. They [the women] had been saying to one another, "Who will roll away the stone for us from the entrance to the tomb?"

(Mark 16:2–3)

Now after he rose early on the first day of the week, he appeared first to Mary Magdalene, from whom he had cast out seven demons. She went out and told those who had been with him, while they were mourning and weeping. But when they heard that he was alive and had been seen by her, they would not believe it.

(Mark 16:9–11)

MARY MAGDALENE
Resurrection

Though the night is still in darkness, I set out for the tomb where my Jesus lies. The air smells of almond trees blossoming, and yet I worry, disobeying Jesus' simple command: "Do not worry about tomorrow." But what about the entrance stone? The soldiers?

An owl screeches overhead, and so close is the sound that I duck. I pray that my Shepherd leads me; I fear I have already passed this bank of olive trees. I listen for Joanna and the others who must be close behind.

A shaft of light escapes the purple horizon, and I see the tomb. The heavy stone that kept me awake worrying is removed. The Roman guards I feared have left their posts.

"Magdalene?" Salome shouts as if this is not her first call.

Joanna locks her arm in mine, and together with Mary, mother of James, we make our way to the tomb and peer inside. Jesus is not there. "Are you sure this is the right cave?" Joanna asks.

But I am staring at the shelf where Jesus' body was laid. Only linen and head cloth remain. "Someone stole the body of the Savior!" I cry. I turn to leave, to search, to get help.

Without a word to the others, I take off at a run. The men are still in hiding, but I will need their help to reclaim the body of Jesus. Soldiers often steal the bodies of the executed and dump them into common graves. I will not allow this.

When I reach the city, heaving, I climb the stairs to the Upper Room and knock. All goes silent. I try the door, but it is locked. "Let me in! I am Mary of Magdala, Magdalene!"

The door opens, and hands pull me in by my forearms. "What is it, Magdalene?" Peter demands. "Were you followed?"

I don't bother to answer him. "We have been to the tomb and found it empty." When no one reacts, I try again. "The tomb of Jesus is empty! Guards are gone, and the stone has been rolled away. Criminals or the guards have stolen the body!"

Someone from the back of the room shouts, "This is why the courts do not allow women as witnesses."

A single lantern casts light on sullen faces showing no interest in what I have just told them. "Do you think I am telling stories? Lying?" Murmurs and nods of agreement travel through the room. Some of these men I have journeyed with for nearly three years, partnered with them, cared for them with every last ounce of wealth I had.

I race from the room, hearing the door bolt behind me. Maybe the other women are still at the tomb. If they are not, I will reclaim the body of Jesus myself.

Pondering . . .

1.) Come up with one-word emotions you might have felt if you had been Mary Magdalene. How many of those emotions have you experienced this week? Ponder each one and what made you feel that way.

2.) Apply the adage *A woman's work is never done* to Mary Magdalene and the other women. Ponder the biblical evidence of loyalty in the women who followed Jesus. Do you consider yourself *loyal*? A hard worker?

3.) In what ways did Jesus' treatment of women counter the culture of the time? Ponder examples when Jesus valued and defended women. How does that treatment apply to you?

4.) Mary Magdalene was so intent on retrieving Jesus' body, she might have missed the miracle of the Resurrection. This Easter, what could you do to increase your wonder and amazement at the Resurrection of Jesus?

Dear God,
Help me be awed and grateful
for your Resurrection.

Day 38

MARY MAGDALENE

Witnesses

When she [Magdalene] had said this, she turned around and saw Jesus standing there, but she did not know that it was Jesus. Jesus said to her, "Woman, why are you weeping? Whom are you looking for?" Supposing him to be the gardener, she said to him, "Sir, if you have carried him away, tell me where you have laid him, and I will take him away." Jesus said to her, "Mary!" She turned and said to him in Hebrew, "Rabbouni!" (which means Teacher).

(John 20:14–16)

So they [the women] left the tomb quickly with fear and great joy and ran to tell his disciples. Suddenly Jesus met them and said, "Greetings!" And they came to him, took hold of his feet, and worshiped him.

(Matthew 28:8–9)

Now it was Mary Magdalene, Joanna, Mary the mother of James, and the other women with them who told this to the apostles. But these words seemed to them an idle tale, and they did not believe them.

(Luke 24:10–11)

MARY MAGDALENE
Witnesses

Filled with anger and frustration at not being believed, I run back to the tomb determined to reclaim the body of Jesus. But before I arrive, John races by me, followed a minute later by Peter. We are close enough that I can see John pause at the tomb's entrance and Peter rush in. After a minute, they both come out, Peter's shoulders slumped as he walks off, John's steps light and his smile deep.

I gather courage and enter the tomb, quickly confirming the absence of Jesus. I cannot stop weeping. Am I to be denied even this, the preparation of the body of my Lord?

"Woman, why are you weeping?" Two men in dazzling white sit where Jesus should be.

"They have taken away my Lord, and I know not where to find him!" I have just finished saying this when I turn and see a man who must be the gardener. "Sir, if you have carried him away, tell me where you laid him, and I will come and bring him back!"

"Mary!"

At the sound of my name, of the voice I know well, my anxious thoughts stop. This is the voice that drew me to him and freed me of my demons. I gaze once more at the One I failed to recognize, and my heart leaps to join his. "Rabbouni!" Though years have passed since I spoke in Aramaic, this name, "Teacher," comes from the depths of my soul. I want to shout for joy, to sing, for the Son of God has allowed me to witness his Resurrection. I cling to him, but he steps back, and I once again receive the smile that touches my soul. "Go and tell the disciples."

I don't want to leave. Yet I am eager to do as my Lord asks. Then as Jesus appeared, so he disappears, entrusting me with such a message of great joy.

I begin my return to the city when I see Salome and the others. In nearly unintelligible words, I tell them our Lord has risen as he promised.

Laughing and crying, we are on our way to Jerusalem when again I hear that voice. "Greetings!"

Fear mixing with joy, we bow down and worship the Son of God. I am aware that he knows how I've sinned, worrying about things I should have trusted him for: the stone at the tomb, the soldier guards, the dark night. By his Resurrection, Jesus has allowed me to see this proof of his forgiveness.

"Do not be afraid," Jesus says. "Go tell the disciples they will again see me."

Glad for our mission, we run to the Upper Room. The minute the door opens, we burst in, all speaking at once, words crashing, exploding on wings of joy.

We are interrupted often: "What?" "What are they talking about?" "Jesus would never choose women as witnesses to the Resurrection, no more than does the Law!"

I can tell the words strike Joanna and Salome hardest. "The law may not trust us," I admit. "But the resurrected Jesus Christ, the Son of God, has made us his first eyewitnesses."

PONDERING . . .

1.) The apostle Paul wrote to the believers in Corinth: *If for this life only we have hoped in Christ, we are of all people most to be pitied* (1 Corinthians 15:19). Why would you be the most pitied if you're only believing in Christ for your lifetime on earth?

2.) How often do you think about an afterlife? How do you picture heaven? This Easter, pray about one person you could talk to about eternal life.

3.) What do you believe is the purpose of the Resurrection? Jesus died for our sins. What if Jesus had only died, but not shown us his resurrected body?

4.) Why do you think the women believed? Why would Jesus have chosen Mary Magdalene and the other women as first to carry the Good News?

Dear God,
Help me celebrate with you this Easter.
Thank you for the joy of the Resurrection.

MARY, MOTHER OF JESUS

Peace

A week later his disciples were again in the house, and Thomas was with them. Although the doors were shut, Jesus came and stood among them and said, "Peace be with you." Then he said to Thomas, "Put your finger here and see my hands. Reach out your hand and put it in my side. Do not doubt but believe." Thomas answered him, "My Lord and my God!" Jesus said to him, "Have you believed because you have seen me? Blessed are those who have not seen and yet have come to believe."

(John 20:26–29)

During the forty days after he suffered and died, he appeared to the apostles from time to time, and he proved to them in many ways that he was actually alive. And he talked to them about the Kingdom of God. Once when he was eating with them, he commanded them, "Do not leave Jerusalem until the Father sends you the gift he promised, as I told you before."

(Acts 1:3–4, NLT)

While they were talking about this, Jesus himself stood among them and said to them, "Peace be with you."

(Luke 24:36)

MARY, MOTHER OF JESUS

Peace

He is alive! My son is alive, and he has fulfilled his mission as the Messiah, the Redeemer, the Savior. For forty days, we have touched him, rejoiced with him, eaten with him, listened to him. So much has happened since Jesus' glorious Resurrection. Judas Iscariot received money from the Pharisees for betraying Jesus, then later took his own life, though my Jesus would have forgiven him. Peter, who three times denied knowing Jesus, has felt the Lord's love and forgiveness. They have even gone fishing together and eaten the fish Jesus cooked!

Thomas, absent from the Upper Room when Jesus first appeared to the disciples, refused to believe Jesus had risen until he saw for himself the nail holes in his Master's hands and touched Jesus' sword-pierced side. A week later—and what a sad and doubting week for Thomas—Jesus showed his wounds to Thomas, who believed and rejoiced. But Jesus reminded him, "Have you believed because you have seen me? Blessed are those who have not seen and yet have come to believe" (John 20:29).

To all of us, Jesus gives what we most need: "*Peace* be with you." When he is with us, I do rest in his peace, and it becomes my own. At times it feels as if we are already on a treasure-filled journey to eternity with him. Even when he is not physically present, he is with me. At last, I understand the name given to him by the angel Gabriel, Immanuel, "God with Us."

Yet clearly, Jesus' mission is not only to give us peace, but to give us purpose. He teaches his disciples continually, meeting in Galilee, Jerusalem, Bethany, mountains and valleys, hillsides and seas. More than once, he has admonished us, "As the Father has sent me, so I have sent you."

At this moment we are gathered beneath the Mount of Olives, near Bethany, where Jesus has led us. We have spent many nights in the home of Martha, Mary, and Lazarus, whose peace and joy are infectious.

Our sister Magdalene, who has lived in near ecstasy since Jesus' Resurrection, is singing. I recognize the words from Isaiah: *Behold, God is my salvation; I will trust, and will not be afraid; for the LORD GOD is my strength and my song, and he has become my salvation* (Isaiah 12:2, ESV).

Scattered on the hillside are the disciples, men and women I have grown to love. We are all waiting.

Pondering . . .

1.) Thomas doubted, even with the testimony of so many he trusted. Do you ever have doubts, even momentary doubts about Jesus or the truth of the Resurrection?

2.) Where do you think doubts come from? How do doubts affect you? What can we do to move past our doubts? How could celebrating Easter and the Resurrection help?

3.) What can you say to a person who admires the life of Jesus and appreciates his example of how we should live but rejects the physical Resurrection of Christ?

4.) With 40 days left on earth before returning to his Father, what would you expect Jesus to talk about and to do? What would you do if you knew you had 40 days left on earth?

Dear God,
Help me trust you more
and to be bold in telling others that
you're more than a good example.

Day 40

WOMEN WHO FOLLOWED JESUS

Purpose

And Jesus came and said to them, "All authority in heaven and on earth has been given to me. Go therefore and make disciples of all nations, baptizing them in the name of the Father and of the Son and of the Holy Spirit and teaching them to obey everything that I have commanded you. And remember, I am with you always, to the end of the age."
(Matthew 28:18–20)

"But you will receive power when the Holy Spirit has come upon you, and you will be my witnesses in Jerusalem, in all Judea and Samaria, and to the ends of the earth."
(Acts 1:8)

After saying this, he was taken up into a cloud while they were watching, and they could no longer see him. As they strained to see him rising into heaven, two white-robed men suddenly stood among them. "Men of Galilee," they said, "why are you standing here staring into heaven? Jesus has been taken from you into heaven, but someday he will return from heaven in the same way you saw him go!"

(Acts 1:9–11, NLT)

When they had entered the city, they went to the room upstairs where they were staying: Peter, and John, and James, and Andrew, Philip and Thomas, Bartholomew and Matthew, James son of Alphaeus, and Simon the Zealot, and Judas son of James. All these were constantly devoting themselves to prayer, together with certain women, including Mary the mother of Jesus, as well as his brothers.

(Acts 1:13–14)

Purpose

MARY, MOTHER OF JESUS

I have known that my son must return to his Father, and now he has. What a joyous reunion for my Joseph, Jesus' earthly father. How I long to be with them! But the Lord has a purpose for leaving me on earth, and who am I to argue?

The eleven apostles watched as Jesus ascended through the clouds. We remain to continue his work and carry to all the nations the Good News of salvation through faith in Christ. It is a staggering task, but Jesus promised that when the Holy Spirit comes upon us, we will be his witnesses, not only in Israel, but to the ends of the earth. The women who have journeyed with Jesus will go. I will go, and Immanuel will be with me.

For I am convinced that neither death, nor life, nor angels, nor rulers, nor things present, nor things to come, nor powers, nor height, nor depth, nor anything else in all creation will be able to separate us from the love of God in Christ Jesus our Lord.

(Romans 8:38–39)

SUSANNA

Once I was frightened by Roman soldiers on horses following me through the markets. When I returned to our camp, Jesus singled me out by the fires, and before I could admit my fears, told me I would never need to fear because now I belonged to him. "You may know the song David wrote that begins, 'God places the lonely in families.'" Jesus swept his arm to include the others in our camp. "You are in the family of God forever, Susanna."

It has taken me a long time to understand, so lacking was I in the experience of belonging and enjoying the security of family. But now I know my fellow believers are my sisters and brothers. I will go where our Father leads.

You received God's Spirit when he adopted you as his own children. Now we call him, "Abba, Father." For his Spirit joins with our spirit to affirm that we are God's children. And since we are his children, we are his heirs. In fact, together with Christ we are heirs of God's glory.

(Romans 8:15–17, NLT)

JOANNA

My husband, dear Chuza, is gone. My sadness at his absence is tempered only by the assurance that I will see him again, as I will see Jesus. Chuza would think this new venture too dangerous for me. But I shall rely on the Lord's strength and protection.

Don't be afraid, for I am with you.
Don't be discouraged, for I am your God.
I will strengthen you and help you.
I will hold you up with my victorious right hand.

(Isaiah 41:10, NLT)

For each day he carries us in his arms.

(Psalm 68:19b, NLT)

SALOME

My boys have told me all about Jesus' ascension, not that they were the only ones there, of course. As James and John strained to see Jesus rising into heaven, two white-robed men suddenly stood among them and asked them why they were staring into heaven. The boys felt rather foolish, and the angels—if that is what they were—said, "Jesus has been taken from you into heaven, but someday he will return from heaven in the same way you saw him go!" That's what they said, and that's what I shall believe through all eternity.

And so I, the Lord's servant, will journey on to tell the world about the glory of the Son of God.

I am your servant; deal with me in unfailing love,
and teach me your decrees.
Give discernment to me, your servant;
then I will understand your laws.

(Psalm 119:124–25, NLT)

MARY OF BETHANY

What an honor to have had the Son of God in our home! And now he has returned to *his* home, to the heavenly Father who sent him. Though I no longer can sit at the Lord's feet and listen to his words, I believe I still *hear* him in my heart and in my soul. I hear him in the Torah and the Prophets, for Jesus the Messiah is the focus of all the Scriptures. I remember his teachings.

Our calling may be here, but Martha, Lazarus, and I will make certain that all in Bethany hear the Good News of salvation in Christ Jesus.

"Do not let your hearts be troubled. Believe in God;
believe also in me.
In my Father's house there are many dwelling
places. If it were not so,
would I have told you that I go to prepare
a place for you?
And if I go and prepare a place for you,
I will come again and will take you to myself,
so that where I am, there you may be also."

(John 14:1–3)

MARY MAGDALENE

Where would I be without Jesus my Savior? He changed me the day he met me, though since then I have needed his forgiveness more often than I had hoped.

I can no longer see my Shepherd, but I am still his sheep. I follow his voice, which comes to me through the Scriptures, through the words Jesus spoke, through remembering. He will never leave me. I will do what he asks of us and be his witness to the world. No doubt, many will not believe, especially the witness of a woman. But this is my mission and my desire, to love the Lord my God with all my heart, all my soul, all my mind and strength. Jesus loved me this way, and he put a new song in my heart. I will tell the world of the Savior's love.

My sheep listen to my voice; I know them, and they follow me. I give them eternal life, and they shall never perish; no one will snatch them out of my hand. My Father, who has given them to me, is greater than all; no one can snatch them out of my Father's hand. I and the Father are one."

(John 10:27–30, NIV)

You thrill me, LORD, with all you have done for me!
I sing for joy because of what you have done.

(Psalm 92:4, NLT)

Pondering . . .

1.) On a scale of 1–10 (10 being absolutely sure) how sure are you that you'll be with Christ for eternity?

2.) What does heaven mean to you? What do you look forward to? Anything "scary" about being face-to-face with Jesus?

3.) Do you believe the Great Commission is part of your purpose in life, to go to all the world and make disciples of all nations? If no, why not? If yes, how can you fulfill that "mission"? Would you talk about Jesus to family, friends, and neighbors ("Jerusalem and Judea")? How about people you don't know or that you consider very different from you ("Samaria")? What can you do to help spread the Good News to "the ends of the earth"?

4.) Which of the women who traveled with Jesus do you identify with the most? Why?

Dear God,
Thank you for loving me as much as you love these brave and faithful women. Help me to take your message of grace and salvation to the whole world.

Now Jesus did many other signs in the presence of his disciples that are not written in this book. But these are written so that you may continue to believe that Jesus is the Messiah, the Son of God, and that through believing you may have life in his name.

(John 20:30–31)

But there are also many other things that Jesus did; if every one of them were written down, I suppose that the world itself could not contain the books that would be written.

(John 21:25)

Afterword

The four accounts of the life, death, and Resurrection of Jesus Christ in Matthew, Mark, Luke, and John never conflict, though sometimes they can confuse. Each Gospel writer tells the truth of what happened through his point of view, his lens: Matthew, the tax collector, focuses on his Jewish audience, recording so many of Jesus' messages and parables and showing Jesus as King. Most scholars believe Mark writes to the Romans, presenting Christ as a man of action and a servant. Luke shows the influence of the Greeks, giving us more details about the believing, faithful women. And John tells us he writes so that the world will believe in Jesus.

All of that can help to explain why some say Mary Magdalene was the first witness to the Resurrection, when a different writer records a group of women who were first to see Jesus. No problem there: they write what matters most to them.

Ponder the last time you met with old friends or attended a conference or a family reunion. If each of you had to write an account of that day, would the reports be identical? Would they conflict because Uncle Pete says Cousin Stella served cookies, but Businesswoman Brianna didn't mention cookies or Stella, choosing instead to tell the fiasco of Uncle Pete's leaky pen? Critics have claimed there are contradictions in the

Gospels: Who was at the cross? Who went to the tomb and in what order? Details can differ without conflicting because we choose which details to record.

If you're in a Bible study, ask each person to write, or tell, what happened at the last meeting. Ask your family to describe last Easter, or Christmas, when you were together. See how your details differ, how perspectives fill in different parts of the story.

I never want anyone to believe that the Word of God isn't true, or that it's full of contradictions. That is a weak argument, sometimes used by a person who doesn't want to face Christ and individual sin. Most criticism of the Bible comes from those who have never read it.

I believe each Gospel account. I've tried to tell the story of the women who journeyed to the cross with Jesus and were the first witnesses to the Resurrection. If I've gotten the details or chronology wrong, don't blame the writers of the Gospels. The fault is mine.

Scripture Credits

are trademarks registered in the United States Patent and Trademark Office by Biblica, Inc.®

Scripture quotations marked (NKJV) are taken from the New King James Version®. Copyright © 1982 by Thomas Nelson. Used by permission. All rights reserved.

Scripture quotations marked (NLT) are taken from the *Holy Bible*, New Living Translation, copyright ©1996, 2004, 2015 by Tyndale House Foundation. Used by permission of Tyndale House Publishers, Carol Stream, Illinois 60188. All rights reserved.

Scripture quotations marked (VOICE) are taken from The Voice™. Copyright © 2012 by Ecclesia Bible Society. Used by permission. All rights reserved.

For Further Study

Bailey, Kenneth E. *Jesus Through Middle Eastern Eyes: Cultural Studies in the Gospels.* Downer's Grove, IL: IVP Academic, 2008.

Bishop, James. *The Day Christ Died.* New York: Harper, 1957.

Burri, René, and H. V. Morton. *In Search of the Holy Land.* New York: Dodd, Mead & Company, Inc, 1979.

Connick, C. Milo. *Jesus the Man, The Mission, and the Message.* Englewood Cliffs, NJ: Prentice Hall, 1963.

Douglas, J. D., ed. *The Illustrated Bible Dictionary*, 3 Volumes. Downers Grove, IL: InterVarsity Press, 1980.

Duvall, J. Scott, and J. Daniel Hays, eds. *The Baker Illustrated Bible Background Commentary.* Ada, MI: Baker Books, 2020.

Edersheim, Alfred. *The Life and Times of Jesus the Messiah.* New York: Longmans, Green, and Co., 1899.

Gower, Ralph. *The New Manners & Customs of Bible Times.* Chicago: Moody Publishers, 2005

Henry, Matthew. *Matthew Henry's Commentary on the Whole Bible*, 6 Volumes. Peabody, MA: Hendrickson, 2014.

Hobbs, Herschel H. *Illustrated Life of Jesus.* Nashville: Holman Bible Publishers, 2000.

Jeremias, Joachim. *Jerusalem in the Times of Jesus.* Minneapolis: Fortress, 2014.

Keener, Craig S. *The IVP Bible Background Commentary New Testament.* Downers Grove, IL: InterVarsity Press, 1993.

Kostenberger, Andreas J., and Justin Taylor. *The Final Days of Jesus.* Wheaton, IL: Crossway, 2014.

Rubin, Rabbi Barry, ed. *The Complete Jewish Study Bible: Insights for Jews and Christians.* Peabody, MS: Hendrickson Publishers, 2016.

Smith, F. LaGard. *The Narrated Bible In Chronological Order, New International Version.* Eugene, OR: Harvest House, 1984.

Tenney, Dr. Merrill C. *New Testament Times.* Grand Rapids, MI: Eerdmans, 1965.

About the Author

Dandi Daley Mackall has spent most of her adult life studying the Bible, leading Bible studies, and writing from a biblical perspective. Her books have won many awards, including the Edgar Award; three Christian Book Awards; Ohio Council International Reading Association Hall of Fame; Amelia Bloom Award for Women; Mom's Choice; NYC Library Top Picks; ALA Best Book. She has received starred reviews from *Publisher's Weekly*, *Booklist*, *Kirkus*, and more, and has been honored to have one of her books become a Hallmark movie. Dandi has written several devotionals for families, novels, children's books and nonfiction offerings including humor and inspiration.

Dandi graduated Magna Cum Laude from the University of Missouri, with a B.A. in foreign languages, later receiving Distinguished Alumna Award. She earned her Master's at University of Central Oklahoma, with the Dean's Art and Achievement Award. Further studies included a year in Hebrew and a year in Greek at Trinity Evangelical Divinity School and courses from the Institute of Biblical Studies. She's taught part-time at Oklahoma University, University of Central Oklahoma, Bethany University, Ashland University in Ohio, Ohio University satellite.

Dandi was a missionary on US college campuses, then became a missionary "behind the Iron Curtain," secretly teaching the Bible to Polish University students, who shared a house with her on the border of Czechoslovakia and Poland.

Currently, Dandi is a national speaker, keynoting at conferences, schools, universities, literary and church events (often about Mary, Elizabeth, and Anna). She's given the Easter address at the Billy Graham Center, the Christmas address at the International Museum of the Bible in Washington, DC, keynoted at the Association of Christian Schools, the Jennings Foundation, and countless library and literary events. She's made multiple appearances on TV, including ABC, NBC, and CBS, and is a frequent guest on radio shows and podcasts.

Dandi writes from rural Ohio, surrounded by her writer-husband, Joe, their three children and their families, plus horses, dogs, cats, a turtle, a tortoise, a chinchilla, and more.

Visit Dandi online at www.dandibooks.com.
Follow her on Facebook:
https://www.facebook.com/dandi.mackall

ABOUT PARACLETE PRESS

Paraclete Press is the publishing arm of the Cape Cod Benedictine community, the Community of Jesus. Presenting a full expression of Christian belief and practice, we reflect the ecumenical charism of the Community and its dedication to sacred music, the fine arts, and the written word.

SCAN
TO
READ

YOU MAY ALSO BE INTERESTED IN

Three Wise Women
40 Devotions
Celebrating Advent with
Mary, Elizabeth, and Anna
DANDI DALEY MACKALL

www.paracletepress.com